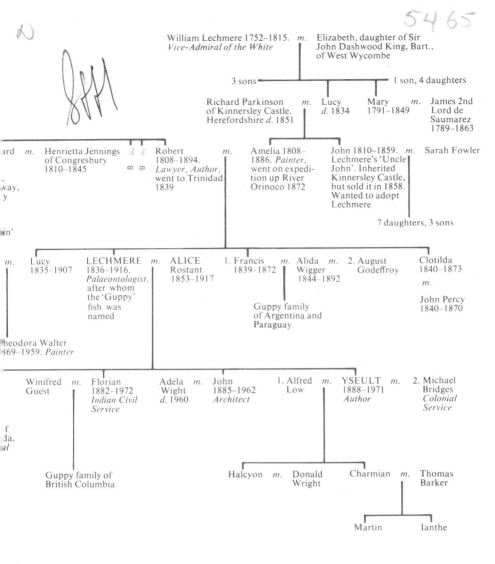

5465

William Lechmere 1752–1815. *m.* Elizabeth, daughter of Sir
Vice-Admiral of the White John Dashwood King, Bart.,
of West Wycombe

3 sons ——— 1 son, 4 daughters

Richard Parkinson *m.* Lucy   Mary *m.* James 2nd
of Kinnersley Castle, *d.* 1834   1791–1849   Lord de
Herefordshire *d.* 1851   Saumarez
1789–1863

...ard *m.* Henrietta Jennings ♂ ♂ Robert *m.* Amelia 1808– John 1810–1859. *m.* Sarah Fowler
of Congresbury ∞ ∞ 1808– 1886. *Painter,* Lechmere's 'Uncle
1810–1845 1894. went on expedi- John'. Inherited
Lawyer, Author, tion up River Kinnersley Castle,
...way, went to Trinidad Orinoco 1872 but sold it in 1858.
y 1839 Wanted to adopt
Lechmere

...in'

7 daughters, 3 sons

m. Lucy   LECHMERE *m.* ALICE   1. Francis *m.* Alida *m.* 2. August   Clotilda
1835–1907   1836–1916.   Rostant   1839–1872   Wigger   Godeffroy   1840–1873
  Palaeontologist.   1853–1917   1844–1892   *m.*
  after whom
  the 'Guppy'   John Percy
  fish was   Guppy family   1840–1870
  named   of Argentina and
     Paraguay

...heodora Walter
...869–1959. *Painter*

Winifred *m.* Florian   Adela *m.* John   1. Alfred *m.* YSEULT *m.* 2. Michael
Guest   1882–1972   Wight   1885–1962   Low   1888–1971   Bridges
  Indian Civil   *d.* 1960   *Architect*   *Author*   *Colonial*
  Service   *Service*

...f
...da.
...l

Guppy family of   Halcyon *m.* Donald   Charmian *m.* Thomas
British Columbia   Wright   Barker

Martin   Ianthe

Errata

Sarah Maria Beach's descendants are
the offspring of her first marriage.

Eugenie ('Nini')   1. Ethel *m.* André Arsène *m.* 2. Louise   Marie *m.* Harry Blackburn Lee
b. 1863   Haughtsen *Doctor* in   *b.* 1870
        London

1 son and 1 daughter

Child of the Tropics
VICTORIAN MEMOIRS

YSEULT BRIDGES

CHILD OF
THE TROPICS

Victorian Memoirs

Edited and completed by
Nicholas Guppy

COLLINS and HARVILL PRESS
London, 1980

ISBN 0 00 262989 5

Set in 11/12 Palatino
by Inforum Ltd, Portsmouth

Printed by T.J. Press Ltd, Padstow
bound by Robert Hartnoll Ltd, Bodmin
for Collins, St James's Place and
Harvill Press, 30A Pavilion Road, London SW 1

Contents

Illustrations

Foreword

My aunt Yseult Bridges, who died on 2 August 1971, achieved considerable success as a writer with her studies of famous crimes: *Saint – with Red hands?* (1954) on the case of Constance Kent; *How Charles Bravo died* (1956) on the extraordinary Balham mystery; *Two studies in Crime* (1959) on the Courvoisier and Wallace cases; and *Poison and Adelaide Bartlett* (1962). These have been adapted many times for television and broadcasting and were reissued again in 1970 by Macmillans.

The present book has never been published before, because in the first instance she felt it to be too personal, and at the same time she regarded it as unfinished. It depicts the rich and fascinating life of English and French settlers in the Caribbean in their Victorian heyday. Perhaps in fiction Patrick Leigh-Fermor in *The Violins of Saint-Jacques*, or George W. Cable in *Madame Delphine* and *Old Creole Days* have captured some of the feeling of that vanished world, but this book is no mere nostalgic evocation. Within the limits of memory each single word is true: the characters are real characters, leading their real lives in the social and political contexts of their times, and some of them are remembered in the history books of today. I have made it my task to check nearly all verifiable facts, so I can vouch for them. The book thus is of some historical interest – as well as being as readable as if it were a novel.

By a fortunate chance among my own papers I have discovered an amazing mass of contemporary paintings,
portraits, photographs, letters, postcards and assorted
souvenirs, such as ball cards and invitations – an unbelievable
treasure trove illustrating almost every person, scene or even
event that Yseult Bridges mentions in this book. These, if not
among my father, Gareth's, effects, were mostly left to me by
the 'cousin Theodora' – Theodora Walter – mentioned in this
book: the grand-daughter of Robert Guppy of Piedmont, and
also of the eminent 19th-century marine artist, Joseph Walter
of Bristol. Theodora was herself a remarkable artist, as these
paintings testify, and she was one of those rare people,
blessed by historians, hated by cleaners, who never throw
anything away.

It has taken me several years to sort, assemble and collate
the objects in this hoard: but they have added to the book
another dimension – that of visual verification – and have
enabled me to fill in with certainty much that might otherwise
have been conjecture.

During my aunt's lifetime I often discussed this book with
her. She would read me extracts, and we would talk about
them at length. As I was born in Trinidad, and brought up
there until 1938, and have since frequently returned, I knew
many of the people and the places mentioned very well, and
these fragments tantalised and exhilarated me, for they
aroused my own fondest childhood memories. Again and
again I would tell her that she must hurry up and complete the
book – little knowing that she had been engaged upon it since
the 1940s, when she began it to relieve the tedium of life as a
Colonial Official's wife in wartime Nigeria.

Trinidad itself is no mere background to this book: 48 miles
by 40 gives no hint of the dimensions of its extraordinary little
world, so varied in beautiful topography and in lively people.
Like only Bali it is one of the nodal islands of the tropical
world, a microcosm that has produced its own rich culture of
dance, music, singing, vivid design and laughter, often strident, always youthful – in which the varied strains of its
mixed bloods meet, clash, and eventually blend. It has given
me a profound sense of pleasure to find that in the works of Dr
Eric Williams, Prime Minister before and since Trinidad's

Independence in 1962, some of my own forebears, the characters of this very work, are singled out, among the Europeans mentioned, for honour and praise for their deep concern for all their fellows of whatever race.

The manuscript of this book was handed to me by my late aunt's husband, Michael Bridges, soon after her death, with instructions to edit and complete it as I found necessary. Throughout I have consulted him, and I wish to thank him for his help, his many kindnesses, and his encouragement. He has given me some short notes about his wife's life which may interest readers:

'Yseult Alice Mary Lechmere Guppy, born 20 April, 1888 in Trinidad, daughter of Robert John Lechmere Guppy and of his wife Alice, daughter of Leonard Rostant.

'Married (1) in April 1906 to Alfred Moore Low, later principal of the Queen's Royal College, Trinidad. Marriage dissolved 1928. Two daughters, Halcyon and Charmian. (2) On 16 August 1932, to Michael Conway Montagu Bridges, Colonial Civil Service, Nigeria.

'She always had an aptitude for writing: During her first marriage she contributed a weekly article on social events to the *Trinidad Guardian*, and once when on leave in England with her first husband she "stood in" for the social correspondent of the *Bystander*. After her second marriage she published a novel, *Questing Heart* in 1934; and in 1936 another, *Red Fruit*, the title of which was changed, to her annoyance, by the publishers, Geoffrey Bles, to *Creole Enchantment*. Both these were set in Trinidad, the latter based upon an original event with a dramatic outcome.

'While in Nigeria she wrote a voluminous monograph on the history, mythology, laws, and customs of the great Yoruba tribe, which aroused the interest of Margery Perham, but unfortunately the only complete copy was lost through enemy action in the Second World War.

'During that war we spent two leaves in the Union of South Africa and she contributed a series of articles to the *Cape Times* on matters of moment at the time. But it was not until we had left Nigeria on retirement that she found her true metier: the full-scale study of notable criminal cases.

'Yseult Bridges died as the result of a fall in her garden at Rye, in which she sustained a compound fracture of the right arm, on 2 August, 1971, at the age of 83'.

NICHOLAS GUPPY

Haddenham
Cambridgeshire
February 1979

CHAPTER ONE

Under the Saman Tree

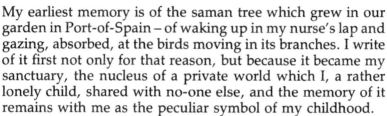

My earliest memory is of the saman tree which grew in our garden in Port-of-Spain – of waking up in my nurse's lap and gazing, absorbed, at the birds moving in its branches. I write of it first not only for that reason, but because it became my sanctuary, the nucleus of a private world which I, a rather lonely child, shared with no-one else, and the memory of it remains with me as the peculiar symbol of my childhood.

The roots of the saman, spreading out in all directions from its mighty trunk, stood out above the ground like the gnarled fingers of a giant hand. The trunk rose straight to a height of forty feet before the branches sprang outward in a wide-spread circle. They swayed and rustled, and sometimes made ominous cracking noises high above our roof, while the long trails of the cat's-claw vine, which festooned them, brushed it with a whispering sound as though the tree were sighing. My mother used to complain of the dripping of moisture from the leaves during the mists of early morning, and sometimes, to my dismay, would swear to have the tree cut down, her resolution hardening as the dripping increased to a gurgling when its fallen leaves blocked the pipes at the onset of the rains – an ugly *fat* sound, I thought like someone being strangled – yet she never carried out the threat because, like the rest of us, she awaited the miracle that took place when the rains ceased. For then the cat's-claw vine would break into bloom overnight with breathtaking suddenness and beauty, every inch of it being closely covered with flowers of the purest gold. Then the air would be heavy with its scent, which

attracted bees and countless other insects, which in turn lured
a host of birds to banquet off that golden service: birds as large
as thrushes of azure blue, golden orioles, and jewel-like
humming birds whose iridescent bodies flashed as they made
their brief darting flights from flower to flower.

I loved that tree at all times and seasons: not only after the
rains when it was at the height of its glory, but also during
those arid weeks before they broke, when its small oval leaves
fluttered down ceaselessly, no longer fresh and verdant, but
sere and dusty. Indeed I think I loved it best then, for I felt it
knew how shabby it looked and was saddened by the knowledge. I shared all my thoughts with it; in its shade I read my
books or gazed up into its branches, lost in day-dreams – in
which I would imagine 'little people' dwelling among its
sprawling roots, with whom I could talk in a special language
compounded of English, French, Spanish, Hindi and Carib
words.

Number 26, Queen's Park West, the house in which I was
born, was a typical town house of the West Indies at that time.
It had probably been built early in Queen Victoria's reign,
together with others in its vicinity of a similar, though not
identical, design, varying like members of a family, each with
distinctive features though obviously springing from a common origin. Single-storeyed and raised some three feet from
the ground on stone pillars, they were built mainly of native
hardwoods and roofed with imported slates. Devoid of
architectural merit, even ugly, yet somehow charming with
their fretted gables and fussy wooden pinnacles, there was
nothing shoddy or mean about them; and they gave the
instant impression of being *homes*.

Our house, larger and set further back from the road than
its neighbours, was approached by a semi-circular gravel
drive which skirted a lawn patterned with formal flower-
beds. A plumbago hedge grew on the inside of a wooden
palisade which divided the compound from the road. A mass
of misty blue flowers for the greater part of the year, it was
clipped to the level of the fence, which made it of a convenient
height to screen the garden and yet allow my mother to see
over it as she sat in her rocking chair on the front porch, from

whence she loved to watch the tide of life that flowed along the white road and drifted across the Queen's Park Savannah beyond, or the high hills and jungle peaks, varying in colour and shadow from moment to moment, that rose encircling its far side.

A wide expanse of unbroken green, in the mornings the Savannah possessed a pastoral charm: dew still sparkled on the grass and trails of mist lingered about the foliage of the great silk cotton, saman and devil's ear trees beneath which cattle grazed, but by afternoon it had undergone a change, taking on a lively urban animation: within its low railings cantered riders on horseback; elsewhere children gathered to fly their kites or play round games; a cricket pitch was dotted with white-clad figures; black nannies, their charges in perambulators, sat gossiping on benches; men and women of all colours and nationalities sauntered along its encircling 'pitch walk', while the island's wealth and fashion drove round it in their carriages.

Government House, set in the Botanic Gardens, dominated the Savannah to the north, and all those houses which overlooked it were regarded as comprising the best residential district in Port-of-Spain, particularly those on the west – as ours was – because they derived the double advantage of facing the prevailing breeze and being shaded from the afternoon sun. To live 'on the Savannah' was in those days the Trinidad equivalent of residing in Park Lane.

The steps leading up to our front door were paved with squares of black and white marble. They were bordered by a low parapet banked with scented maidenhair ferns, so luxuriant in growth of fronds that their earthenware pots were completely hidden. Panelled doors a full ten feet high opened into the front porch which, like the rest of the house, was enclosed with slatted jalousies and casement windows, kept half closed during most of the day so that the interior was drenched in a cool green twilight that it was a relief to enter from the glare outside.

To my childhood's eyes our drawing-room was immense and very beautiful. Even grown-up opinion accounted it large and its furnishings handsome. Its polished mahogany floor was a shining mirror. On its walls hung a number of water colours in dull gold frames – two or three by David Cox whose pupil my grandmother Amelia had once been – with here and there an engraving framed in black and gilt beading. A crystal chandelier hung from the centre of the ceiling, while the armchairs and Chesterfield sofa had been purchased during a visit of my parents to England, soon after their marriage, from Maples in London.

The arrival of that suite had created something of a sensation in Port-of-Spain, for apart from Government House, there were few households in Trinidad, about the year 1870, which could boast a suite of upholstered furniture brought out from England. Every friend, every relative, every social rival of my mother had called to see, to admire, or to envy it. The very pensioners, protégés and dependants on her bounty were ushered from their place of congregation, the back verandah, to behold, to exclaim at, and to praise the splendour of the suite from that unimaginable Elysium, 'Maples in London'.

With the passing of the years the tapestry with which it was upholstered grew faded, but subsequent visits to 'Maples in London' provided a succession of loose covers in the latest designs. There was one set which my mother prized particularly: not without complacency she would inform her visitors that it was the latest 'Morris design'; and when, as not infrequently happened, that magic name seemed to touch no responsive chord, she would add helpfully, 'William Morris, the Pre-Raphaelite, you know' – an explanation which seldom contrived to dispel the mystification.

Nor did it dispel mine. Somehow I must have associated the name with Raphael's religious pictures, for I was convinced that the Pre-Raphaelites were a monkish order over whom William Morris, in hood and cowl, ruled as a kind of abbot. Perhaps I was not so far from the truth.

Hot and exhausted from games outside, how often would I slip into this room and cast myself upon the floor, panting. Then I would pass into a state of exquisite dreaming: the cool green shade became the depths of the sea, the twining flowers and trellises of the Chintzes exotic growths of the ocean bed. The reflected lustres of the chandelier were silver fish nosing past my arms and legs and brushing my cheeks coldly; the diving girl who stood upon a pedestal was a mermaid fair, who told me stories of drowned sailors and lost argosies and treasure; and the whole dim room became a wonderland of fantastic submarine adventures . . .

One of the largest rooms in our house was my father's study, and here he spent the greater part of each day engrossed in one or other of his many interests. Its walls were lined from floor to ceiling with bookshelves and cabinets containing his specimens. In the centre of the room was his writing-table, everything on it arranged with symmetrical neatness. His microscope was placed under one window, his telescope at another. Later he built a tower with a sliding roof to house the latter, which I learned to manipulate while I still had to climb on to a high stool in order to look through it.

When I first remember my father – I was the youngest of the family – he had resigned his official post of Chief Inspector of Schools, in which, over a period of twenty-three years, he had reorganised the school system of the island. Scientific studies he pursued with unfailing zest and he was also finding other new outlets for his creative energies. One of these consisted in founding in Port-of-Spain, at the time of Queen Victoria's Golden Jubilee (1887), the Victoria Institute, an educational institution inspired by and upon similar lines to the London Polytechnic, the founder of which, Quintin Hogg, was a personal friend of his. For years as president he carried on its administration as well as taking an active part in its educational functions.

Another enterprise of his was the *Trinidad Almanack*, which he and his brother Francis had founded in 1866. Similar in conception to *Whitaker's*, it contained much the same diversity of information, and quickly established itself as the standard book of reference. After his brother's death for many years he produced and edited it single-handed, until with increasing age, he found this too much and the Government took it over and adopted it as the official year book.

When my father was occupied in his study it was understood that he was not to be disturbed, but an exception was made in my case and I entered whenever I pleased – though at a very early age I realised that I was enjoying a privilege which must not be abused; an understanding which my father fostered in his own inimitable way. I remember an early instance: I had trotted in and seated myself on the floor near his writing table where he was at work, and soon was asking:

'What are you writing, Daddy?'

'I'm working on the almanack. I'm calculating the rising and setting of the sun and the phases of the moon.'

'Is it very important?'

'Very. I must stick to it like wax.'

'Why?'

'Well, for one thing they must be accurate. A blunder might result in my making the sun rise at midnight!'

'How?'

Patiently he explained.

'I see. It *is* important. Then I mustn't talk or ask questions.'

'It would certainly *help* if you didn't.'

After a pause in which I pondered what he had said I acquiesced in this reasoning but inquired optimistically:

'Just every *now* and *then* may I say something?'

'Well . . . *only* every now and then, though I'd much rather you waited until I'd finished.'

So I learned, even when some question was burning on my lips, to refrain from putting it until he laid down his pen and asked with one of his twinkling smiles:

'Well, Little Lass, and now what paradox have you to propound?'

To write of my father truthfully is a task beyond my powers – emotion blurs my vision. Even now, when I am approaching the age at which he died, I still relive the hours I spent with him in close companionship, and every expression that flitted across his countenance springs vividly to my mind. Perhaps no-one can describe someone he has loved and admired so completely: to catalogue his virtues is to risk making him seem priggish, to ignore them, to rob him of the qualities which were his essence: learning and wisdom, gentleness and strength; great personal charm, yet forthrightness; in a complex, subtle, yet transparent character.

All he undertook he accomplished with zest and perfection; he loathed deceit, disloyalty, dishonesty; and did not hesitate to express his hatred of cant. He held that all men should find in work well done its own reward, and the fact that he found few people who shared these same standards disappointed and even saddened but never embittered him – for he also possessed the saving grace of humour.

His collection of marine fauna and his geological discoveries in Trinidad brought him considerable esteem in his lifetime and a recognition that continued to grow, so that after his death even his slighter papers were collected and published by Cornell University Press under the title of *A Reprint of the more Inaccessible Palaeontological writings of Robert John Lechmere Guppy*. At the age of eighty he died, retaining to the end a freshness which made any meeting with him a delightful experience.

One of his friends, Judge Russell, wrote a long light-hearted poem about him which was published after his death (A.D. Russell *Legends of the Bocas*, London 1922), inspired by a lecture he gave on Atlantis – he had written a serious memoir in the *Geological Magazine* on a possible Atlantis in the Early Tertiary period, long before man had appeared on earth. This poem begins:

'Go you not near the rock, my child! Go you not near the isle!*
The man of Eld inhabits there, and he will you beguile.'
'What would he do to me, father? What would he do to me?'
'He'd weave you legends old and strange, and tales of grammarye:
Legends and rhymes of bygone times, and things so long ago,
The world has forgot if they're true or not, and it's better to leave them
    so.'
'What is the old man like, father?' — 'Like a rock in its mossy bed;
For he sits so still that the birds at will may rest on the dreamer's head.
He's shrivelled and shrunk like a gnarled trunk, and never a word says
    he,
Till the spell is broke by the little folk that cluster around his knee,
With their tricks and their smiles, and their simple wiles, and voices so
    clear and so shrill.
Not a word can he hear, but they tickle his ear; and he'll laugh to himself
    and weep,
And laugh again, like the sun and the rain; and he's off with his tales,
    until

* Referring to Little Gasparile, Gasparillo, or Guppy Island, as it was variously called, which at one time belonged to my father (c.f. page 82)

The moon is high in the eastern sky, and the little ones all asleep.
. . . He tells them tales of dragons and whales, and countries under the
*   sea,*
And a continent all wrecked and rent; and he waves an ancient chart,'
. . . 'See, see,' cries he, with elfish glee, 'there great Atlantis lay;
That mighty power — and in an hour it all had passed away!
. . . 'It was a lovely place, I ween, and its end was wondrous sad;
'There's nothing of it left,' quoth he, 'save only Trinidad!'
When the chasm broke, and the whole world shook, at the reft of that
*   ruinous breach,*
It slipped off like a lizard's tail, and wriggled away out of reach.
'It wriggled away out of reach,' quoth he, 'and curled right up in a knot;
'That's why one side is an anticline, and the other side is nought . . .
'It's a very deep matter, that,' quoth he, 'and wants a lot of thought!'

Which shows that I was not alone in succumbing to his magic.

Next to my father's study was his workshop. Here he spent
the early hours of each morning at the carpenter's bench
where he made bookshelves, cedar-lined cabinets for his
specimens, as well as all sorts of articles for household use. He
made chairs and tables for me, suitable to my size, also my
doll's-house and the Lilliputian furniture within it. In the
workshop he was accessible to everyone and as he sawed and
planed, in short sleeves and an old pair of drill trousers, he
would sing *I Dreamed that I Dwelt in Marble Halls*, *A White Sheet
and A Flowing Sea*, *Pop goes the Weasel* or *Poor old Joe* and other
plantation songs of the American 'deep South'.

I would join in with my high treble as I built houses with the
bits of wood he had sawn off, making hills and valleys about
them with sawdust, or caught the long fragrant shavings as
they fell from the plane and pretended that they were families
of snakes. I could chatter as much as I liked now and ask a
thousand questions, to which he would sometimes return
nonsense answers.

'What's that you're making, Daddy?'

With a mischievous twinkle he would retort:

'A wigwam for a goose's bridle', or 'A cobweb ladder so that
the wind can climb up to reach the stars', – although he never
failed eventually to explain what the thing really was.

Once, fixing the long shavings about my head with pins, I ran in to display them to him as he planed a plank.

'Look, Daddy! Look at my golden curls!' I cried – for my hair was straight and lank, and I longed ardently to possess flowing curls.

I must have looked a grotesque little object, but with the gravity with which he responded to all my moods he paused and slowly considered the effect.

'Um-m-m. Very nice indeed. Very curly curls . . . But, you know, attractive though they be, I like your own hair best.'

'*Do you?*' I cried delightedly. 'Do you really and *truly*? Everybody says my hair is like rat's-tails.'

'Everybody says a great deal of nonsense! I shouldn't pay much attention to what everybody says if I were you.'

'But it's so hard not to . . . I should like to be *very, very* beautiful with hair falling like a cloak about me,' I said, quoting from some story I had been reading.

Peering along the edge of the plank with one eye closed, he murmered; 'Crooked as a dog's hind leg'; then again gave me his full attention.

'Hair falling like a cloak? . . . Picturesque perhaps, but wouldn't it be hot in this climate? You'd find it a nuisance, I fancy. What a job combing and brushing it, and how painful getting the tangles out! Beauty is a matter of degree. For instance, you said the other day that you preferred the delicate shapes and tints of some of my smaller shells to the bright rainbow colour of the big mother-of-pearl shell in which I keep my paper clips. Would you want every flower to be a rose?'

'Oh *no!*' I cried emphatically, 'It would be dreadful not to have the forget-me-nots and all the lovely tiny flowers!'

'Well, there you are then! Do you suppose the forget-me-nots want to be changed into roses? They have their own beauty and don't envy the rose at all.'

Thus he would resolve my discontents and put me in a good humour with myself.

By ten o'clock of a morning he had oiled his tools and put each in its proper place. Then he bathed and dressed and retired to his study, to begin the more serious work of the day.

At four o'clock, after I had had my 'dinner' and was ready to go out with Estelle, my black nannie, it was understood that I should present myself to him.

'Time for Combies,' I would announce, and he would lay down his pen and regard me seriously:

'Time for Combies, is it? And how many are due today?'

That might cause me to ponder as I recalled some misdemeanour which ought now to be confessed, but of which I might be uncertain whether he knew or not. A blameless day was rewarded by five of Huntley and Palmer's Combination Biscuits, the number being reduced for the more glaring acts of naughtiness.

'Only three,' I might murmur ruefully.

'Not a very good day in fact?'

'N-n-no.'

'Pity! . . . Ah well, there's so much good in the worst of us and so much bad in the best of us . . .'

He would take the large square tin from its shelf and hold it on his knees while with small agonies of indecision I made my selection. Dominoes, with pink icing and white dots were really my favourites, but the Crowns were more 'important' – I was quite sure that Queen Victoria had personally commanded Mr Huntley and Mr Palmer to make them. So, though not quite so delicious as the Dominoes, they nevertheless ranked higher. Three Crowns and two Dominoes were the reward of a perfect day.

In the evenings my father used to sit in a long chair in the drawing-room beside a round mahogany table on which were placed the books and periodicals he was reading at the time. His reading lamp stood on it, too, the wick carefully trimmed.

This was the hour between my supper and my bedtime, and it was the time for playing games of make-believe with him. Sometimes I would pretend to be a *marchande*, and with a tray balanced on my head and my frock hitched over a cord as the *marchandes* hitched their skirts I would enter the room crying shrilly:

'*Poisson! Poisson*! Fresh fe-e-eesh! . . . Yo' wantin' any fresh feesh dis marnin', Massah?'

He would have some coloured counters ready in his pocket with which to pay me, but I would remonstrate if he failed to bargain in the local fashion.

'You're not playing *properly*, Daddy! You must say it's too dear. You must beat me down. The *marchandes* think you've no sense if you don't. Do play properly!'

He would laugh at that, and promise. And sometimes he would introduce unexpected variations into these games which were full of fun, causing me to laugh delightedly, so that my mother would glance at us and exclaim:

'Listen to those two! That child's laughter is the most delicious sound.'

My father might also vary our programme by reciting some curious old rhyme of which he had many stored in his memory. This was one:

> *A man of words and not of deeds*
> *Is like a garden full of weeds,*
>
> *And when the weeds begin to grow*
> *It's like a garden full of snow,*
>
> *And when the snow begins to fall*
> *It's like a bird upon the wall,*
>
> *And when the bird begins to fly*
> *It's like an eagle in the sky,*
>
> *And when the sky begins to roar*
> *It's like a lion at the door,*
>
> *And when the door begins to crack*
> *It's like a stick upon the back,*
>
> *And when the back begins to smart*
> *It's like a penknife in the heart,*
>
> *And when the heart begins to bleed*
> *You're dead, dead, dead indeed!*

Another, which I used in the 'counting-out' games I played with other children, was evidently a corruption of one of the old vernacular tables used by shepherds in counting their sheep:

> One-ery, two-ery, dickory, seven,
> Araby, crackery, ten and eleven
> Tin, tan, dusty Dan,
> Tweedledum, tweedledee, twenty-one.

It was said of my father that he had taught himself to read at the age of three. I was certainly not much older when I did the same, and entirely self-taught. Books overflowed everywhere – the older novelists, works on science, philosophy, history, religion and the classics, beside poetry, drama, and the popular fiction of the day, a selection of which arrived from time to time in a great box from Mudie's. The volumes on the shelves in the study alone were diverse enough to provide a liberal education.

I had the run of all these books and often plunged into those which were far beyond my understanding. Many were the words which I could not pronounce at all and whose meaning was completely obscure, but this did not deter me in the least, so long as I could get the general drift of what the book was about.

My mother indulged in yellow-backed French novels and the lighter English fiction, over which she could often be heard to chuckle and sometimes be seen surreptitiously drying her tears. She was also a devotee of Tennyson and possessed the edition of his works illustrated by Gustave Doré. *The Idylls of the King* and *The Princess* appealed so particularly to her romantic nature that she named three of her children Gareth, Florian and Yseult – myself.

We also subscribed to the *Strand Magazine*, *The Illustrated London News*, *Punch*, and, strangely enough, to that delightfully vulgar weekly, *Ally Sloper*. How well I remember its illustrations of bulbous-nosed tipplers with top-hats askew, and girls in tights with the fashionable hour-glass figure, all of which gave much scope for my colouring powers.

I had intended to give no more than a brief description of our tropical home, but memories have taken possession of me, and I am still little further than the workshop. I must write too of the back verandah, which was the hub and nucleus of our domestic life and of the relatives, servants and retainers who composed our household, and try to convey something of the warmth and friendliness which pervaded it . . . I am apt to get lost among my memories and swept along by their surge – forgetful that you who read this cannot feel deep within you the long-remembered rhythm of those days.

CHAPTER TWO

My Mother Alice

———◦❦◦———

Although my mother was not endowed with the beauty which distinguished her elder and younger sisters, Anna and Eugenie, she was extremely pretty and possessed great natural charm. Her vivacity and quick responsiveness made her a fascinating companion, while the warmth and generosity of her nature attracted all sorts and conditions of people. She made friends quickly and kept them long, and those men who had been her admirers in youth remained devoted to her throughout their lives.

She had nine children in all: six sons – one of whom died in infancy – and three daughters. Her first child was born when she was eighteen, and her last – myself – when she was in her thirties.

Like all Frenchwomen of her class and period her notions of life were matriarchal. She ruled her servants despotically, and although she was over-indulgent to her children she plotted their future with more regard to her own ambitions for them than to any consideration of their own wishes. Her idea of a perfect old age was typically French: to have all her children living under the same roof with her, along with their husbands or wives, providing her with an unending source of interest and an unlimited supply of grandchildren.

She was never so happy as when she was engrossed with the intimate problems of other people, whose joys and sorrows she eagerly made her own. She was as sincerely concerned with the troubles that afflicted some old coloured retainer, as deeply stirred by the misfortunes of some distant and degenerate relative, as stimulated and entranced by the intrigues and rivalries of Trinidad social life, as she was absorbed in the affairs of her immediate kith and kin. Her elastic mind was charged with subtleties, and she enjoyed nothing so much as an opportunity to deploy them, the seemingly artless character of the exercise masking its intrinsic skill. Entirely urbane in outlook she fell an easy victim to *ennui*, and constant companionship was essential to her.

How did it come about that two such people, seemingly so utterly different as my mother and father, should have fallen in love and married? He, as uncompromisingly English and intellectual as she was profoundly French and instinctive; he scholarly, shunning society, while to her the social round was the breath of life? An early photograph of my father, taken in 1847 when he was eleven (and one of the earliest known using my grandmother's friend, Fox Talbot's, method) tells some of the story: the sadness in those young eyes speaks of the loneliness that he and his brother and sisters felt, brought up in England, far, far away from their parents – a loneliness that affected my father all his early life, until he had the good fortune to meet this woman of surpassing warmth; while my mother's passionate nature had yearned for someone worthy to idealise. From the moment they met they were hardly apart – and though so much younger, she died within a few months of him. Their marriage was not one of interest or on any superficial level, but of *love* pure and simple – and totally successful. And this despite a most fundamental point of difference – for all her life my mother was an ardent Roman Catholic, while my father was Protestant to his deepest core. It was a condition of the Church of Rome in mixed marriages that the children be baptised in that faith. My father complied because he scrupulously honoured pledges. But he bitterly resented being subjected to such coercion and it prejudiced him permanently against the Roman Communion. And it is somewhat ironic to record that of his eight children only two – my two sisters – remained members of the Roman Church after early childhood.

Nothing had been further from my father's mind when he first arrived in Trinidad, aged twenty-two, than to stay there. It was his intention to return to England to pursue the study of

Natural Science. But he was in an unsettled state of mind as a result of some remarkable adventures.

He had passed his childhood and adolescence at Kinnersley Castle, in Herefordshire, living with his mother's father, and had been educated there by various tutors. On his grandfather's death he continued to live there, but now the situation changed – for his uncle, John Parkinson, who had inherited the property, seems to have fallen completely under his spell, and to have made him virtually a prisoner.

John Parkinson had been disappointed in his children: none had any character or ability, he would declare, whereas Lechmere had the Dashwood fire, like his own beloved sister! The notorious founder of the Hellfire Club had been his great-grandfather's brother, and there were still strong family resemblances in looks and temperament.

The idea became obsessionally fixed in his mind – that Lechmere must study estate management and run the property, of several thousands of acres and many farms, on his children's behalf. He would make Lechmere his chief heir . . .

Lechmere was appalled where almost anyone else might have been delighted. He resented plans being made for his future: he wanted to see the world; he was already corresponding with eminent scientists and he wished to pursue a career in academic science.

In 1852, when he was sixteen, his father's mother died at Clifton, near Bristol. She had married again after Samuel Guppy's death, but her much younger second husband, Charles Eyre Coote, was estranged from her family due to his insatiable love of gambling, which eventually reduced them both to semi-dependence. Now with her dead, Lechmere had nowhere to escape, and he seems to have fallen into a state of deep gloom and isolation.

Then unexpectedly, when he was eighteen, he received a handsome gift from a great aunt's widowed husband, the second Lord de Saumarez, and with the independence this gave decided to leave his uncle and go to Oxford. He was actually awaiting an interview with the master of his father's old college when a series of letters arrived from Kinnersley, imploring him to return.

Had he been left alone he might have done so. Instead he

left Oxford immediately and took ship for Australia – the furthest possible point away from his doting uncle!

Once he had arrived there, he embarked almost immediately again on a ship for Tasmania, where he spent a few weeks; then sailed on for New Zealand – at which point he vanished, for over two years!

In despair his parents and his uncle advertised for news of his whereabouts – his uncle to the effect that if he did not return by a certain date the castle would have to be sold; and indeed it was, in 1858.

Lechmere meanwhile had been shipwrecked on North Island, New Zealand, and had been living very happily amongst the Maoris who had rescued him, roaming the hills and forests, collecting specimens, and thoroughly enjoying himself. Although this was the time of the Maori wars, they had treated him with great hospitality, and to the end of his life he loved to talk of his adventures with them, and to display the tattoos on his back – of various designs, including a sailing canoe, and on his wedding finger – a ring! He had left only just in time, he declared, to avoid marrying the chief's daughter! No, my mother would stamp her foot, he must have actually been married to her! – at which his eyes would twinkle.

He had remained with the Maoris until, from a newspaper that was brought to him, he judged that it was safe to return. Then he made his way to the nearest English settlement, took ship for England, and thence to Trinidad. (His diary of this adventure was unfortunately lost in Trinidad during the Second World War, when my brother Gareth's belongings were removed from storage in the Government buildings, the Red House.)

To begin with he had gone to stay with his parents and his brother Francis, who were living in San Fernando, in the south of the island. Then he had taken a temporary job in the Government Service which required his living in Port-of-Spain. He was greatly interested in education, and his seriousness of mind was evident, so before long the Trinidad Government had invited him to organise and establish an educational system, which he gladly accepted.

As his duties took him about the island, he had opportunities in his spare time for studying its geology and marine shells, fossil and living – his two principal scientific interests; and it did not take him long to discover what a virgin field Trinidad was. Soon he was collecting other specimens and sending them to his correspondents in England. And this is how it came about that he sent specimens of the tiny 'Millions' fish, which he found in the St. Ann's river near Port-of-Spain, to Dr. Albert Günther of the British Museum, who named it *Girardinus Guppyi*. Although this fish is now scientifically *Poecilia reticulata*, popularly it has been called 'the Guppy' ever since, and it has become the world's most widely kept tropical aquarium fish, and has been introduced throughout the warm regions of the earth to control mosquito larvae. My father would have been delighted that his descriptions of fossil *foraminifera* (a form of microscopic floating life) would be used in future times for the diagnosis of oil-bearing rock strata, but I think he would have been totally amazed and highly amused that this tiny fish would cause his name to become a household word, and to pass into the dictionary to join that select band of private individuals whose names have attached to popular articles, like Mrs Bloomer or the Earl of Sandwich.

He was still intending to return to England when he was asked to be Best Man at the wedding in San Fernando of his friend Robert Fitzsimmons, to Anna, the eldest daughter of Leonard Rostant, of a French family long settled in the island.

A path linked Piedmont Cottage, his parents' home with La Coulée, the Rostant home, for a deep friendship had sprung up between the two families. Leonard Rostant had married Arsène, daughter of Charles Maingot, head of another French family, and the musical talents and happy dispositions of their four daughters were renowned, and made any visit to their home enjoyable.

At the wedding my father had met Alice, the second daughter, for the first time. He was then thirty-three, she a school-girl of sixteen with a pair of fine brown eyes, a shower of dark hair rippling down to below her waist, and a quick spontaneous smile which displayed very perfect and very regular white teeth. It seems that they fell deeply in love immediately.

And at this very time the Government offered to appoint

my father as permanent head of the Department of Education, which he had done so much to create. To accept would mean that he would be able to marry at once. So he did – and within a few weeks of my mother's seventeenth birthday on 20th January 1870, their marriage had taken place. Thenceforward Trinidad became their home.

Every afternoon at four o'clock Samuel, our 'yard-boy', passed the polishing broom over the drawing-room floor to remove any dust which might have settled during the day, while Lavinia, the parlour-maid, having wiped over the furniture with the same intention, threw open the jalousies and front door, and drew my mother's rocking chair to a position just behind the threshold.

From this vantage point my mother could enjoy the refreshing breeze which blew across the Savannah, and, lorgnettes in hand – for she was very short-sighted – could catch a first glimpse of callers, so that when their carriages turned in at the gate, and with a crunching of hooves on gravel drew up at the steps, she would be ready, as the visitors alighted with a rustling of silk petticoats and billowing of gauzy skirts, to greet them in exactly the manner she deemed the circumstances required.

Her smile was always in evidence, but its quality, the angle of her handshake, the whole poise of her body, were nicely adjusted to correspond with the social distinction of the visitors and the degree of cordiality she felt towards them. Some might receive a kiss, but even these kisses could express a wide range of feeling, varying from what my father called a 'social bite' or a disapproving peck to an affectionate salutation on both cheeks.

Formal callers were ushered into the drawing-room, their visits never lasting more than the prescribed quarter of an hour, and the conversation being confined to generalities. Friends and relatives, however, sank into chairs on the porch itself, and my mother reseated herself in her 'rocker'. The atmosphere was *intime* and time was disregarded. As the chatter grew confidential chairs would be hitched closer together: voices might sink to tense whispers, broken by smothered exclamations or shocked little gasps.

My father seldom emerged from his study until visiting hours were over. Friends of his own, after paying their respects to my mother, would join him there. Yet, although he had nothing in common with my mother's more frivolous acquaintances, he nevertheless admired pretty women and delighted in their company. Some were great admirers of his, so that, when they called, my mother would send Lavinia to tell him of their arrival and he would come and bask contentedly in the sunshine of their smiles, instantly assuming an air of constraint if, as sometimes happened, he felt my mother was growing jealous.

One of the particular pleasures of my childhood was to watch the final stages of my mother's dressing when she was going out calling. Her absorption was complete as she studied the line of her hat and set it at its most *chic* angle. With the aid of a hat-pin a wave of hair would be more smoothly arranged, or a curl induced to lie more becomingly on her forehead. Standing before her cheval-glass she would turn this way and that, her capable little hands with their sure, deft touch settling the folds of her skirt, giving a tug of adjustment to her bodice, before deciding on the right place to pin a brooch or a flower. Then with a last, lingering glance over her shoulder at her reflection she would tap her way on her high heels to the porch, her maid, 'Truda, following with her freshly powdered white kid gloves, her fan, card-case, and lace parasol.

Seated in her rocker, there would then ensue the ceremony – for it was a ceremony – of pulling on her gloves: the tips of the four fingers were inserted first and the glove coaxed and smoothed over them; then, with the thumb curled into the palm, the glove was brought over the hand, the thumb inserted and worked in, and with a series of small tugs the whole was brought neatly into place and the tiny mother-of-pearl buttons fastened.

But in spite of her apparent concentration on this task my mother's thoughts would be actively engaged with other matters, and her glance would be sharply scrutinising her immediate surroundings. The corners of her fine large eyes would be contracted, the line of her lips taut, if the call she was about to pay was upon someone who had managed to earn her displeasure. One could see her mind carefully coining the exact phrases with which adroitly to convey to the delinquent the enormity of her behaviour. On the other hand she might be looking forward to seeing a new baby, or a friend whose recent return from Europe would yield an absorbing discussion of fashions and theatres on the one hand and local affairs on the other. In that case fleeting smiles would come and go about her lips and mirth would flicker in her eyes as she sorted out little quips suitable to the occasion.

As she swung gently to and fro in her chair she was critically alert to notice, through her lorgnettes, whether Samuel had polished out a smudge on the floor or if Lavinia had left a trace of dust on a table. Reassured on these points she turned her attention to the garden. Had the steps been scrubbed until they were spotless and properly polished with coconut oil? Were there weeds in the drive? Had it been freshly raked? . . . Convinced at last that everything was as it should be she would relax with a sigh of satisfaction and await the arrival of the carriage. As soon as this drew up Lavinia would appear to settle her comfortably into it with a cushion at her back, then open and hand her the parasol.

My mother always took a friend with her when she drove out, partly because she liked having someone to talk to, but principally because, hating the necessity of using her lorgnettes upon the occupants of each passing carriage she needed someone to prompt her as to whom she should bow and to whom she should not. Never had she driven alone since the occasion – the mere thought of which still made her hot with shame – when she had bestowed one of her most gracious bows and warmest smiles upon a notorious lady of the town.

So at the approach of each carriage the companion would take a hurried glance and hiss in my mother's ear: 'Bow, dear, bow!' and obediently but blindly she would bow to the passing blur, anxiously inquiring: 'Who is it? Who is it?' At other times the companion would warn sharply: 'Look the other way, Alice! Don't bow for goodness sake!'

My mother had tiny arched feet and slender, shapely legs. My father took the greatest pride and pleasure in her whole appearance, but her exquisite little feet were his particular delight. All her boots and shoes were made for her by Pinet, of Paris, all were hand-sewn of finest *glacé* kid in either black or bronze, and all had rounded toes and Louis Quinze heels. My mother used to bewail the fact that he would not permit them to be made with pointed toes, as was the fashion, and when, as the result of *Trilby*, the long, narrow foot became the rage she bewailed it more than ever. But my father denounced the fashion as calculated to deform the foot, for crowded toes, corns and bunions were objects of horror to him, and his own feet were as free from distortion as my mother's. He also took care to see that his children's shoes were properly fitting and encouraged us to run barefoot about house and garden. To him I owe the fact that my own feet are without blemish.

In an age when women's stockings were exclusively either black or white he realised the attractions of coloured ones, to match the dress, and these he also got from Paris for my mother. These stockings were of silk with embroidered clocks, and with them came many pairs of garters – dainty creations in various colours, ruched with ribbon and trimmed with minute hand-sewn flowers. Those were the days when garters were 'correct', but suspenders were considered 'fast': ten years later this order had become reversed and garters were stigmatised as 'suggestive'.

Early in my childhood we all paid a visit to England of which I remember little except that at the end of it my three elder brothers, 'Jim' (Plantagenet), 'Fitz' (Percy) and Gareth, and my eldest sister, Enid, remained behind at school. Fitz I never saw again, for he became a mining engineer and went to Mexico and then California, where he remained for the rest of his life. The other two came back on the completion of their education and entered the service of the Trinidad Government. Jim had inherited my father's scientific proclivities. He undertook research for the Natural History Museum in South Kensington and wrote a number of papers on Trinidad fish and insects. These he illustrated himself, each of his plates being a work of art. He was an early advocate of the biological control of insect pests, which he applied successfully to the sugar-cane frog hopper. He was co-founder of the Trinidad Field Naturalists' Club. His nature was a singularly happy

one. Like my father he cared nothing for social occasions, but
unlike him he took life uncritically. He devoted his leisure
hours to sailing a small yacht called *Vanessa Io*, with the
assistance of a crew that consisted of a single elderly negro
who had sailed the seven seas and rejoiced in the name of
'Tobago John'.

Gareth was his exact opposite. He had no scientific leanings
and, like my mother, was emotional, affectionate, generous
to a fault and a lover of social life. Good-looking, with great
charm of manner, scrupulously particular about his appearance, he was a perfect dancer, a notable bridge player, and
good at golf and tennis.

Of all her children Gareth was the one most in sympathy
with my mother. Complete confidence existed between them.
She was familiar with his most intimate affairs; the older she
grew the more she clung to him, and through his successes or
frustrations in love or work she relived her own youth and
kept her mind flexible. She would weep away her anxieties on
his shoulder, or, with him sitting beside her rocker, laugh
delightedly at his stories. He was the only one for whom she
did not plot marriage, for, although she would never have
admitted it, she could not have borne to share his love with
anyone else. Gareth, though impulsive and quick tempered,
was extremely popular because his sincerity was so obvious
that he was readily forgiven even by those he had most hotly
challenged. He 'warmed both hands before the fire of life' but
resolved never to marry so long as our mother was alive. Nor
did he.

My eldest sister also returned to Trinidad, married and
settled down there; but I saw little of her. At the time of which
I am writing only my second sister, Ruth, myself and the two
boys, Florian and John, who were between us in age, were at
home together – the boys attending the Queen's Royal College. Florian, the elder, a born student, reserved and aloof,
was resentful of any interference with the kind of life he liked
to lead. Like my father he shunned social occasions, even
children's parties as a boy, and his principal enjoyment consisted in leaving the house at dawn with a knapsack of sand-
wiches, disappearing into the hills and only returning at
sunset. As soon as dinner was over he went to his room where

he remained immersed in study until he went to bed. He was head of his school at an unusually early age and passed the Rhodes scholarship examination while he was still a year too young to be eligible for the scholarship itself.

Everyone predicted a brilliant future for him and it was decided that he should enter the Indian Civil Service. I doubt if this were the career he would have chosen had he not been subjected to pressure, and it soon became apparent that the constraints and artifice of Indian official life were uncongenial, so that as soon as he could he retired on pension and, purchasing an island near Vancouver, settled down with his wife, their young family, and the works of Plato, to the untramelled existence which suited his temperament. Of John I saw little, because he was away from home a great deal.

The nine years which divided my second sister, Ruth, or 'Imp' as my father called her, from me, constituted too wide a gap for either of us to bridge successfully, and so, left very much to myself, I was the lonely one in our family. Yet I studied Ruth closely. I was small and thin, with a pale, pointed face, a pair of hazel eyes, a rather *retroussé* nose, a sensitive mouth, and straight, lank hair. My sister was very different. She was said to resemble our grandmother. Slender and long-legged, quick with life and intelligence, she had a mercurial temperament, at one moment charged with a brittle gaiety, and the next capricious, petulant or withdrawn; but in all moods and at all moments lovely to behold, with golden eyes and a mass of tawny hair which sprayed out in crisp waves and tendrils about her heart-shaped face. To her, dancing was a vital need, and in dancing she would express her every emotion.

My earliest conception of life was of being lost in the shadows beyond Ruth's radiance. I was not jealous of her, for I was proud of her and as fascinated by her as were our parents themselves. But I longed with all my heart to be like her, and among the roots of the saman tree I tried to imitate her lissom dancing – until, observed and teased, I gave up. But most of all I wanted to have hair that curled like hers.

One night after being put to bed I got up and twisted my hair tightly and agonisingly into curlers and, to make assurance doubly sure, coated it generously with gum arabic. As the gum dried I began to feel as though I was being scalped, but I reminded myself that one must suffer to be beautiful. So I tossed in restless discomfort throughout the night, and when at dawn I peered anxiously at myself in the mirror I was horrified at the spectacle that confronted me. My hair was caked in a congealed mass, as stiff as a board, and my eyebrows were drawn half-way up my forehead.

I was dumb with chagrin and disappointment. I quailed before the thought of the laughter that would follow discovery, so in despair I sought out Estelle, my nurse, who, when she had recovered from the shock my appearance caused her, clasped me in her arms and wept. Together we mingled our tears while I beseeched her to help me and tell no-one what I had done. But even after a prolonged and painful process of soap and hot water, lumps of the matted hair had to be cut away before the curlers could be removed, and my mother's cry of dismay when she beheld me led to the whole story being told.

My attempts to be like Ruth ceased after this. I decided that it was in every way less painful just to be myself, and to accept with philosophy the fact that visitors were apt to turn eyes of open admiration from Ruth to regard me somewhat compassionately, while they murmured that they were sure I was a clever little girl; or, in less sanguine tones, that my looks might improve as I grew up. More and more frequently I was dubbed 'quaint' and 'old-fashioned', and with a child's aptitude for coming to terms with the inevitable, grew to accept the state of affairs with decreasing perturbation, learning to depend more and more upon my father's company and upon my books, and day-dreams among the roots of the saman.

There I would relate and re-enact, with minute descriptions, every experience I underwent to the audience of my 'little people', regaling them with conversations, imitations and anecdotes. For I was happy-natured, with an essential gladness of spirit, which welled up within me over so many aspects of the natural world: at the flawless blue of the sky, at its velvety darkness pricked over with stars; at the sun shining through a passing shower; at the sight of heavy raindrops making tiny fountains where they fell; at the scent which arose from the rain-soaked earth. I would stand entranced by the gentle tints of lichens and mosses, or the delicate fashioning of the gills of a mushroom. With a similar felicity and completeness I could identify myself with the characters of the books I read so that I lived their very lives, and with equal ease galloped wildly through Windsor Forest with Herne the Hunter on his 'swart Horse', voyaged the seas as Mr Midshipman Easy, or became Jo in *Little Women*.

CHAPTER THREE

Early Morning

———⋙∘◉∘⋘———

The waking of our household was an ever fresh delight to me.

While it was still dark I would hear Samuel chopping the kindling to light the first of the row of charcoal braziers in the kitchen. Then would come the sleepy, dragging steps of 'Truda as she shuffled along the covered way from her room across the compound. I knew just how she would stretch her arms high above her head as she gave a prodigious yawn, just how her cotton frock would strain over her big bust and then relax as with a shake of her fat hips she brought her fists to her eyes to rub the sleep from them.

'Gawd! I'se well weary! . . . De marnin' does strike too chill 'pon a pusson straight from she bed,' she would complain, clucking her distaste in her throat.

Her feet would thump up the wooden steps of the back verandah and next I would hear the scrape and rasp of the key being turned in the lock of the back door. Ponderous footfalls would announce her departure to the kitchen with the coffee-pot in which the coffee had been filtering all night, and which was now to be heated up on the brazier which Samuel had lit. When it was boiling she would put it on a tray with two cups and saucers and a bowl of sugar and take it to my parents' bedroom. I would hear the muffled sounds of their greeting to her and the tinkle of the brass rings as she drew back their mosquito net. That was my signal. Instantly I would spring out of my bed, scuttle along the passage and scramble into theirs demanding: 'Coffee-sugar!'

'Good morning Little Lass' my father would say with a

deep chuckle, and my mother would incline her cheek for a kiss. Then a spoonful of brown crystals steeped in coffee – a *canard* or *bonne bouche* in my mother's language – would be handed to me by my father with a saucer and the injunction to 'mind the drops' as I sucked and crunched.

Curled up between them I would lie snugly while they sipped their strong black coffee and spoke with comfortable desultoriness of the needs of the day. The world outside was still held in a grey crepuscular twilight, and the room filled with strange shadows beyond the golden radiance of the lamp on the bedside table. From all around came the crowing of cocks, some shrill and quavering, some hoarse and cracked, others deep and challenging. A dog or two would be barking, while in a muted accompaniment came the pulsating chorus from millions of tiny insects whose voices had whirred and hummed since night had fallen. As the first rays of dawn began to melt the darkness above the hilltops they would gradually lapse into silence and give place to the chirping and fluttering of birds as they stirred and shook themselves in the branches of the saman.

Now along the white road the scavenger's cart was coming.

'Whoa-a back!' he shouted to his mule, and his shovel scraped the road's hard surface. 'Gee-whee-e-e!' he cried, and on the mule plodded.

'Truda was now opening the drawing-room. She would sweep around the walls first, then, pushing back the furniture, the centre of the room.

'The castors of that Chesterfield are squeaking again,' my mother might protest.

'Then we must give them a dose of *castor* oil,' my father would answer, looking at me slyly as he perpetrated the pun.

'Truda was now padding about polishing the furniture, and I knew that at this moment the gangling form of Augustus Bellborder, the collar of his old jacket turned up against the chill of the early morning, would be shambling through the back gate. He would go straight to the kitchen and stand shivering on its threshold, the picture of misery, until Cook – fussing to be off to market – handed him a steaming mug of coffee sweetened with both condensed milk and brown sugar. He would drink the scalding stuff in great gulps, smacking his thick lips in loud appreciation, until its stimulating warmth flowing into his attenuated body at last provoked that startling grimace which was his idea of a smile.

The solemn ceremony of polishing the drawing-room floor was about to begin. Samuel – who was Augustus' henchman while this operation lasted, and at everybody else's beck and call for the rest of the day – was busy mustering the polish, cloths and broom. In a few moments came a harsh sound as Augustus and Samuel, down on their knees, rubbed on the polish with coconut husks. It was followed presently by the regular '*click* . . . *swish* . . . *click* . . . *swish*' of the lead-weighted broom with its rotary hinge being pushed forward and pulled backwards over the floor until it attained the flawless perfection which was Augustus' pride.

My brothers would now be tumbling out of bed and scampering along the covered way to the plunge bath. Lavinia would be laying the table for *petit déjeuner*, which was always eaten on the back verandah. The homely sounds of domestic activity were merging and mingling in increasing volume. Drawing his heavy gold watch from under the pillow my father would say:

'Off you go Little Lass, – it's getting-up time.'

In fact it was rare for me to linger in my parents' bed long enough to be given this warning. So many things were calling to me with the rising of the sun, that I must be out . . . *out*! Already I knew that no passing moment could ever be recaptured, and not a fraction of that fresh dew-spangled hour before the day's heat began must be lost.

I would slip into my room and hurriedly pull on my clothes. 'Hurry! Hurry!' I would admonish myself, fearful lest Estelle should come and catch me. First a little liberty bodice buttoning up the front, to which my brief drawers were fastened. Next the first frock that came to hand – so long as its top button was done up, what did the others matter? Hurry, *hurry* or she would insist on hair-combing and tooth-brushing.

'Finished! Hurrah!' Then out I slipped, eyes and ears alert for any impending presence. Though if I encountered Estelle now I knew that I was pretty safe from capture – she might flounder vainly in pursuit, protesting breathlessly: 'Come back, Miss Baby! Come right back! . . . Yo' hair aint comb!' But

I could outrun her any day.

If I escaped detection, now there were certain rituals to be observed: I must run the length of the narrow cement water-channel, which protected our roses from leaf-cutter ants, without overbalancing; then with eyes shut I must walk from it across the drive to the edge of the lawn. There, if the first hibiscus bloom I saw on opening my eyes was pink or yellow, I would have a happy surprise in store for me; if white or red, then my next wish on catching a falling leaf would not be granted. After thus determining the omens, I would go to the front gate. Out in the Savannah the cows were cropping the coarse grass, under trees which I knew were stretching their branches after the night's sleep. They slept, so Estelle had told me, not as we sleep, helpless and exposed, but resting from growth; and when the moon was waxing they did not sleep at all, for then their sap flowed faster and if you leaned your forehead against their trunks you could sense its tingling current.

At this hour the blue flowers of the plumbago hedge were the same frail colour as the thin mist which still trailed gauzily among the clefts and valleys of the hills to the north. Dew silvered the lawn, making jewelled lace of the spiders' webs. It drenched the flowers, washing them free of the dust of yesterday and endowing their bright colours with a glistening purity. Among the branches of the saman the birds flirted and chirped. Its branches reached out high overhead, and as I perched myself on the culvert outside our gate its leaves came gently down as the breeze stirred them, and I would try to catch one to make the day's wish. I disregarded the chill and dampness of the culvert, for I, the cows and the bright birds, had this fresh world to ourselves.

Then, as the prison clock in the town struck seven, all the cooks from the houses along the road began to emerge to wend their way to market. Their heads tied in gay bandanna handkerchiefs, their long skirts gathered between their hands in front to keep them out of the dust, their baskets on their arms, they would exchange noisy greetings as they mustered in a procession. Walking not side by side but in a straggling single file – perhaps a habit born, generations before, in the forest paths of far away Africa – their voices and quick gusts of laughter were pitched high so as to carry up and down the line. I knew most of them, and these all had a word for me:

'Look 'pon Miss Baby! She never comb she hair! Mus' be she ran away from Estelle dis marnin'!'

'Eh-eh, Miss Baby, dat place be too cold fo' yo' to res' 'pon! Yo' will be takin' a fever, sure t'ing.'

Often they would have some small gift for me, usually fruit – a golden balata, a luscious *pois doux*, or a spray of scarlet gree-grees – and I would give them a rose or hibiscus flower which they would tuck behind an ear; or a few beads or a coloured plate from a magazine, for them to pin up in their rooms.

Even before the last of the cooks had gone by, nannies would be appearing with their charges for the morning's outing – bonnetted babes in high perambulators or tiny tottering toddlers – and assemble in gossiping groups. Then my brothers would come pelting out of the house to join the throng of boys on their way to the College. Hardly had they gone than Ruth set out for her school. Although she was now old enough to dispense with the attendance of a servant, it was not considered 'correct' for girls to go about by themselves, so, by mutual arrangement between their mothers, the girls of our neighbourhood collected at the corner of Tranquillity Avenue (later renamed Cipriani Boulevard) and went on in a body.

Tranquillity Avenue, despite its name, was a lively thoroughfare which ran townwards from the Savannah only a short distance from our gates. It was here that the quaint little trams, each drawn by a pair of mules, and looking with their open sides like toast-racks on wheels, waited to collect their passengers: for 'catching the morning tram' was the Trinidad equivalent of catching the commuters' train.

By now another troupe had appeared upon the scene: this consisted of the *marchandes*, or vendors of foodstuffs, both male and female, who in my childhood were one of the features of Port-of-Spain, their cries, revealing Trinidad's cosmopolitan origins, as characteristic as those of London and, like them, now extinct.

'Poisson! Poisson! Fresh Fe-e-esh! Fresh Fe-e-esh!' chanted the fish vendor.

Chinese market gardeners, wearing their native dress and carrying their produce in two baskets slung from either end of a bamboo pole borne upon the shoulder, ambled along at a jog-trot, calling:

> 'Pima pepper, cucumbo-o-o,
> Okolo-o-o-o-,*
> Tomato-o-o-,
> Water kyssle' **

'Turtle-eggs! Turtle-eggs!' heralded the approach of negroes trundling barrows of this delicacy from the sandbanks of the Orinoco: lightly boiled, a hole pinched in the parchment-like shell, and some grains of salt and pepper inserted, they were then squeezed down the throat. When the season for turtles' eggs was over the same vendors hawked plantains – a large, coarse variety of banana, excellent boiled or fried:

> 'Tan banan,
> Four fo' five cents, Madam!'

'Oy-si-ta! Oy-si-ta!' The Trinidad oyster, though smaller than those of England – one can eat three dozen – is unsurpassed for delicacy of flavour. The trade in those days was entirely in the hands of the Chinese, and their principal vendor, Silam Achee, became immensely wealthy – at three pence a dozen!

The *marchandes* also hawked dried meat, known as *tassasalé*, cakes and sweetmeats, and live poultry which they carried in wooden trays balanced upon their heads.

Not only negroes and Chinese, but East Indians with their donkey-carts, also had a place in the morning procession: charcoal, for the kitchen braziers, and green coconuts were the wares in which they specialised. The water of the green coconut is sweet and nutty, and alleged by those who ought to know to be the finest tonic for the kidneys.

All the while this varied cavalcade has been passing before my mind's eye I have pictured myself sitting on the damp culvert outside our house in the chilly mists of early morning. In fact I seldom lingered there after the cooks had gone by, for

---

* Okra
** Water-cress

by then I would have heard Estelle calling me:

'Miss Baby! Miss Baby! Where yo' be? Yo' be bad chil', whom no pusson caint do nuttin wid! Come, let me 'range yo' decent befo' yo' payrents see yo'.'

At which I would sprint to the back verandah regardless of the consequences. There would be my parents sitting at the table whereon were bowls of fruit, coffee and hot, appetising-smelling crisp little loaves of bread. At the sight of my untidiness my mother would fling up her hands in horror and appeal to my father:

'Lechmere, just look at Baby! Her hair hasn't been brushed and look! . . . her frock's not even buttoned up! She's a disgrace!'

'I couldn't reach to fasten more than the top button,' I would protest feebly.

'And what, may I ask, is Estelle employed for but to do up your buttons?'

'She does, Mother . . . I mean, she would . . . but she's so *slow* and I *had* to get out.'

'*Had* to get out? Don't be ridiculous! I've never known a child with such notions.' Then she would appeal to my father: 'I wish you would use your authority, Lechmere.'

Such an appeal put my father in a dilemma. He understood, as I knew full well, what it was that impelled me out of doors before anyone else was up.

'Little Lass,' he would say gravely, 'you must do as your mother wishes in these matters.'

I would bite a finger-tip and murmur disconsolately:

'I simply can't *bear* waiting for Estelle! It's *miserable!*'

Then he would smile and say:

'You can at least make yourself tidy before you go out – run and do so now.'

Afterwards when, sweetly docile, I had submitted myself to Estelle's attentions and given her a hug, peace would be restored between us and I would become again 'her own sweet darlin' '.

CHAPTER FOUR

The Back Verandah

As was usual in a Trinidad house in those days the back verandah was the centre of domestic life and activity.

At one end of ours, near steps down to a covered way which connected the main house with a wing containing the plunge-bath, kitchen and servants' rooms, was the pantry. Here stood a big safe of wire gauze, to keep out flies, its four feet in pans of paraffin to exclude ants. On its shelves were kept the stores in daily use, and beside it stood a sack of coffee beans, a pan-full of which was given each morning to the cook to be parched and ground, and during the process the whole compound was filled with fragrance.

Here, too, was a big store-cupboard, its shelves filled with all those delectable things my mother considered essential to good cooking, and close by a large ice-chest for which ice was delivered daily. At the opposite end of the verandah was the linen room, with a square deal table at which Mrs Laycock sat to do the mending and making.

Except for a railing the verandah was open on to the back yard: in the middle stood a table where at 8 a.m. we had our breakfast, *petit déjeuner*, or 'marnin' tea'. Then when this meal was over and its debris cleared away, the verandah assumed a different character. It became, so to speak, thrown open to the public. The *marchandes*, swinging in through the back gate, brought to it their trays of fowls and ducks, their calabashes of eggs. 'Truda would go off and tell my mother:

'Madam, a *marchande* come wid fowls.'

My mother would absent-mindedly ask a series of

questions to none of which she paused for a reply:

'Fowls . . .? Do we want any fowls? Are they good birds? Young and plump? Have you examined them . . .?'

With the composure of one who knows that the wheel of household affairs will revolve smoothly without any great effort on her part my mother would complete what she was doing, then tap her way with quick, short steps on her high heels to the back verandah and glance down at the tray of panting fowls, their feet tied tightly together.

' 'Truda, have you examined these fowls?'

'Yes, Madam; dese t'ree be good.'

The *marchande* would praise them all and, producing a hanging scale would dangle it, ready to pass the hook through the string about the feet of the birds 'Truda had chosen, then hold it up so that my mother could read the weight.

'Very well, I'll take those. How much do they come to? . . . 'Truda, give them to Samuel and see that he cuts their wings before loosing them in the run, and tell him to give them water – *clean* water, mind – and some food.'

By nine o'clock Cook would have returned from market with a basket containing 'the greens' on her arm and followed by her 'porter' – a boy carrying the heavier basket with the 'white vegetables', the ox-tail that went into the stock-pot every day, the meat and the fish. All she had bought would be washed and arranged in bowls and dishes upon the table on the back verandah. There were always plantains, avocado pears, christophene, lettuce and water-cress, and I can remember seven different varieties of fresh beans which could be bought in the market at different seasons of the year. The 'white vegetables' included potatoes, yams, dasheen, tannia, eddoes, artichokes, topitambos* and sweet potatoes. When Cook had set out her purchases 'Truda would summon my mother that she might inspect, approve or criticise, and give her orders. Then back through the house the high heels would tap their way.

'Those lettuce leaves are bruised, Cook. I don't like them like that. And those bouquets of herbs are *very* small – only *one*

---

* The nutty rhizome of *Calathea allouya*

sprig of thyme in each and a few absurd little chives!'

'Eh, Madam, de *marchandes* all be sayin' de thyme be well scarce.'

'Nonsense! Just as much thyme is grown now as there ever was . . . That looks a nice fillet. Now, mind your charcoal fire is *quite* clear and *red* when you grill it. 'Truda give Cook a tin of black mushrooms for the fillet; and, Cook, see that you put *plenty* of parsley in the butter and that the fillet is *piping* hot when it comes to table. The parsley butter must be only *just beginning* to melt on it – not *running* but *firm*.'

Instructions having been given concerning what my father called 'lunch' and everyone else, in the French tradition, 'breakfast', and which was always at noon, and for dinner at half-past seven, my mother departed once more.

Now had come the hour when pensioners, protégés and parasites began to drift in and seat themselves on the bench near the pantry door. The pensioners who were old servants either of my mother's family or of my father's, came not only to collect their pensions but to regale my mother with news of themselves and their descendants, and to indulge with the unembittered melancholy of the old and simple in memories of days gone by, now shrouded in a golden mist, contrasting past contentment and present tribulation. Their interest in our affairs never flagged. The news of even a minor family affliction evoked genuine distress and instant offers of service; a piece of good fortune wreathed their faces in smiles and made them clap their hands. The fabric of their lives had been so completely interwoven with our own that death alone could sever the thread. They were honourable, loyal and gentle, and even they would bewail the fact that their own children's children – who sometimes accompanied them, grinning shyly – would probably never acquire the grace and strength, the manners and skills, that such a relationship could bring. I hope that their like have not gone for ever.

My parents' protégés were many. Some were descendants of deceased pensioners who had made their own way in the world and were attached to us only by bonds of sentiment. Some had been placed in domestic service on my mother's recommendation; others had gained posts as teachers at one of the Government schools through my father's influence.

No. 26 Queen's Park West. The Saman tree is behind
the house on the right

Alice's drawing room

Alice with daughter Enid and Enid's daughter Ruth
on the front verandah

Yseult on her donkey Greycoat, with Samuel the yardboy

Lechmere Guppy in 1892

...and in 1847, aged 11, one of the first known
photographs using Fox Talbot's method

The 'Guppy' fish (1. male, 1a, female—natural size 1½")
originally named *Girardinus Guppyi*,
discovered by Lechmere when he was 23
from a painting by Plantagenet (Jim) Guppy

1a.

Every now and then they presented themselves to 'pay their compliments' and to inform my parents of the state of their affairs.

While the protégés were worthy and respectable, very different were the parasites. Whining wastrels, mostly half-castes and poor whites, outcasts often from families which had been intimate with our own, they were mutually contemptuous, yet had this in common: the knowledge that no tale of woe ever failed to solicit alms from my mother. One exercised a macabre fascination over me, for I knew that his family still lived in the old style and were prodigiously proud of the name they bore, while he existed in a state of penury and squalor; and I wondered what terrible misdeed he had done to be so relentlessly rejected. All the signs of years of dissipation were stamped upon his ravaged features, but despite jerking hands, shifty glance and hang-dog look he still contrived to retain some traces of an original handsomeness and gentility of manner.

These people aroused my father's fury, for they represented a side of things that he despised, so naturally they took every precaution to avoid him, only sneaking into the compound when they had made certain he was out of the way. And my mother's benefactions were equally surreptitious. But occasionally, as was inevitable, he learned of their visits, and his indignation was unbounded:

'Mendicancy and mendacity!' he would explode. 'Beggars and liars! How do you expect to reform parasites by encouraging their parasitism? If he can get what he wants this way, why should he ever become a decent person?'

But no remonstrances ever checked my mother's charity. She would turn aside my father's wrath with a soft answer and continue as before, and though she would look worried and sad for a while whenever she found out that her generosity had been abused, she would usually manage to find some excuse for the culprit.

It was often difficult to tell the age of the negroes. Often intuitively wise, to many of them time was a mere abstraction, and advancing age did not concern them or lessen their zest for life until they began to feel its leaden hand. They seldom knew how old they were – 'Me mudder make me de year de cholera be so bad. Dat be long-time, and I feel so well-weary when de night come I mus' be well old.' And that was about as near as they ever got to it.

'Zabette, one of the most dearly loved of our pensioners, must have been well over a hundred when she died. A child of one of the domestic slaves in the household of my mother's grandfather Leon Toussaint Rostant, she had been born shortly before Emancipation. As was frequently the case she had grown up as the playmate of the master's children. Later she had suckled the child of her white foster-sister with one of her own. In due course she had taken over control of my grandfather's domestic staff, had acted as midwife to my mother at the birth of her first children, and returned after each of these confinements to dwell again in my grandfather's household. In her room in his compound she lived in peace and dignity with all her wants provided, while the pension she received gave her an added independence. She spoke of my mother and her sisters as 'me white chillun' and her own as 'me black fambly'.

Once a week 'Zabette would spend a morning on our back verandah, which she dominated as imperiously as she had dominated the household of my mother's parents. Her sharp-sighted eyes looked out from her wrinkled face with an intensity that was almost hypnotic. Our servants trembled before it. They regarded 'Zabette with superstitious dread, for she was known to be able to 'work Obeah'.

I myself once had an instance of the powers that were attributed to her. I was due to sail for British Guiana (now Guyana) on an expedition to the Kaieteur Falls – no mean undertaking in those days – and on the eve of my departure went to take leave of 'Zabette, by then completely bed-ridden and so old that she looked like a tiny shrivelled monkey. By chance I mentioned that I had lost a diamond and opal brooch, which had disappeared mysteriously from my dressing-table one evening. After a long silence, in which she lay with closed eyes, she told me when I got home to summon all the servants and tell them that I had informed her of my loss. 'Tell dem', she said, 'dat I, 'Zabette, know which person have t'ief dat brooch, and I is gwine put Obeah 'pon dem.

Dey's gwine get de belly-ache too bad till de day yo' find it, an' will dead if you don' find it. Now, chil', in two weeks you find it.'

When I got home I did as she had bidden, but although I narrowly watched the faces of the assembled group their expressions revealed nothing.

After reaching British Guiana we spent two or three days in Georgetown, then, proceeding leisurely by train and river launch, reached Rockstone as the evening fog from the Essequibo was closing opaquely about the rest-house. This was where we must begin to take quinine to prevent malaria. I got the bottle and emptied some of the powder into the palm of my hand preparatory to filling a gelatine capsule with it. I noticed that the box containing the capsules was oddly heavy and, opening it, saw that there among them lay my brooch. It was just fourteen days since I had seen 'Zabette. When we returned to Trinidad I learned that one of the yard-boys had been ill with severe internal pains for two weeks after we left and on his sudden recovery he had hastily packaged his belongings and disappeared. But how he had managed to slip that brooch among the capsules remains to me as much a mystery as 'Zabette's supernatural powers.

'Zabette also had an instinctive knowledge of the medical properties of herbs and other substances. She cured our coughs with a syrup she made by boiling together the flowers of the double scarlet hibiscus, elder blossoms, dark brown sugar and the essential oil which she extracted from orange-rind. Her hot bush baths, to be followed by a cup of hot bush tea which had been drawn in a quassia cup, were renowned for bringing down a high temperature in cases of fever.

Once my sister Enid's small son of three years lay dangerously ill with vomiting and diarrhoea. Hour after hour he grew frailer and weaker and his temperature mounted. 'Zabette asked the doctor if she might try a cure of her own, and he, knowing 'Zabette and being beside an old man who had experienced the strange knowledge that resided in people such as she, readily agreed. I watched her grind into a fine powder a number of ugly little whisps which she produced from a phial and moisten the powder with a few drops of a liquid from another phial. She sat by the child's bed in withdrawn silence, her fingers on his pulse, while from time to time she placed a pinch of the mixture on his tongue. By evening he had kept down half a teaspoonful of chicken jelly. All night 'Zabette remained, silent and immobile, at his bedside, giving him a tiny portion of chicken jelly and a pinch of powder at intervals. By noon next day the diarrhoea had abated and in a couple of days the fever left him.

The whisps were the dried skin which lines the gizzards of fowls, and which I believe, are rich in pepsin; the fluid with which she moistened the powder was her own special decoction of witch hazel. 'Zabette always wore the style of dress common among the negroes brought up in French families, which was known as 'Martiniquan', being generally worn by the women of that island. It consisted of a short-waisted, tight-fitting bodice with a 'V' neck and puff sleeves, to which a long, full skirt was gathered. A kerchief, folded in a triangle was brought over the shoulders and pinned below the 'V'. Another kerchief bound the head, the two corners being knotted in front to give a gay 'butterfly' effect. It was a distinctive and becoming attire and young women carried it out in vivid colours wearing strings of bright beads with it, and earrings. 'Zabette's outfits however, were of unrelieved black with never an ornament of any kind.

Our servants seemed to be able to anticipate a visit from 'Zabette with uncanny foresight, and they then behaved like a military detachment about to be inspected by the G.O.C. They all busied themselves with something, and whatever they found to do, did as it were at the double – and conspicuously. Samuel would grasp the knife-board and a handful of knives, and squatting down in a prominent place, set to work with a will; 'Truda would rush into the pantry, snatch up all the glass cloths within reach, and then take up her position at the sink in the yard to be discovered soaping and rinsing energetically; Estelle would suddenly discover a rent in a frock of mine and ensconce herself on the doorstep of her room with the work-basket, making a great display with its contents. Even Cook, who was a superior person with a status above the rest, would apply herself to some such task as beating up eggs, which could be done in the kitchen doorway.

At all this sudden commotion in the house my mother

would chuckle and say: ' 'Zabette must be coming!' And then 'Zabette would appear, leaning on her stick, perhaps with the other hand resting on the shoulder of a great-grandchild, while Princess, her eldest daughter, followed at a respectful distance like an A.D.C. Slowly, majestically, she advanced, her penetrating glance lingering for a moment upon each servant in turn, while they bowed low and murmured obsequiously: 'Marnin', Mamzelle 'Zabette; I pray Gawd I see yo' well?' To each she gave a brief inclination of her head as she stalked on towards the ancient Windsor chair which had been placed on the verandah for her, and into which she subsided while her attendants seated themselves behind it on the bench.

'Zabette knew all the tales which her ancestors had brought from Africa, where they had been related for countless generations, and which the slaves in the New World translated into the languages of their masters: Br'er Rabbit and Br'er Fox of the Southern States of America being in Trinidad Compère Lapin and Compère Tigre. As told by 'Zabette these old stories were dramatic *tours-de-force*. Enthralled, I listened as her hollow growls proclaimed the hunger of Compère Tigre, and with a delicious thrill I watched her lick her chops as he considered what a savoury morsel Compère Lapin would make. In what suspense I held my breath when 'Zabette cringed and trembled, and I knew that now Compère Lapin had heard the savage roar which announced that his relentless enemy was on his trail; and with what a gasp of relief I saw the cunning glint in her eyes as Compère Lapin devised a means of outwitting Compère Tigre and of putting him to scorn before all the beasts of the forest. Although I knew that Compère Lapin was bound to triumph in the end – he always did – 'Zabette's dramatic art kept up the tension until the swift climax came, when her pealing laughter proclaimed Compère Lapin's triumphant derision, and I would bounce madly up and down squealing my delight.

Or again 'Zabette might elect to talk of 'de ol' times,' and I would sit on the little bench my father had made me and gaze up into her withered old face with its network of wrinkles as she told me about the balls my French great-grandparents had given at Brothers Estate, to which the Governor had come in state, and how the slaves had lined the drive with *flambeaux* in their hands to light the way; how they had stamped their feet in time to the songs they sang as the carriages rolled by; how they had been given demi-johns of rum to broach and goats to roast whole as they gathered around a great fire outside their barracks, and how they had danced all night to the drums while 'de whitefolk' up at 'de House' had trodden more stately measures to the music of the orchestra.

'E-e-e!' she would cry, clapping her hands and shaking her shoulders in a rhythmic motion to the tune in her memory, her eyes afire with a brief recrudescence of the warm blood of youth. 'E-e-e! dem was de days fo' true! E-e-e . . .!' Then the dark shadow of time and change would come stealing into them, quenching that sudden brilliant glow, and her hands would fall limply into her lap as she muttered contemptuously: 'Dese-here folk dese days aint knowin' what livin' is – dey be poo' trash!'

Thompson was another of our pensioners who must have attained a great age. Even at the time of which I am writing, when I was still a child, he was already bent with the weight of years, and he lived until after I was married and had children of my own. He was the embodiment of all that was best in mankind: gentle, patient, faithful, with the most perfect manners and the essential sweetness of the pure in heart.

He came each Monday to receive the allowance my father made him. For his long years of service as court messenger at San Fernando – the court over which my grandfather had presided – and afterwards as porter and caretaker at the Victoria Institute, to which my father had been instrumental in appointing him, a munificent government had awarded him the princely pension of £12 per annum, which even by the values of those days could not have kept him from starvation.

He would take his seat on the back verandah with a deep sigh of contentment, placing his carefully pipeclayed helmet and stick on the floor beside him, and his smile would grow wide and his eyes light up as a mug of hot, sweet coffee was handed to him. Sipping it with relish he settled down to enjoy an hour or two of conversation, first with my parents and then with whomsoever came his way. After my parents' deaths he came to me for his pension, and he would gaze upon my small daughter with his age-dimmed eyes and his sweet smile, and murmur melodiously. 'Four generations o' de fambly I done see. Me time 'mos' finish now.'

Lavinia, 'Truda, Estelle, Cook and Samuel formed the inner circle of our domestic staff, but its outer ramifications extended further and included Mrs Laycock, Laycock her husband, Jimmy their son, Augustus Bellborder, Lizzie Waldron and, last but not least, Mary Hodge.

Mrs Laycock was a mulatto: very tall, very thin, she was the most lugubrious person I have ever known, her long face stamped with an expression of enduring melancholy. Never did she smile or display the slightest trace of animation. Her voice was so low that it was little more than a whisper. When spoken to she stood with her hands clasped together and her eyes downcast in an attitude of humility which would have done credit to Uriah Heep. The only mode of self-expression she allowed herself was to crack her finger-joints in a volley of sharp reports. Her duties were those of a general help and sewing woman and she always comported herself as though there had been a death in the house.

Laycock was the very opposite of his wife. A stocky, full-blooded negro of middle age, he was cheerful and talkative. He was our general handyman, doing all the repairs, painting and plumbing that the house needed. His occupations provided me with endless diversion: he would arrange his planks as a see-saw for me; he would allow me to stir his paints, or to fish about in his tool-box and hand him the tacks, nails, screws and staples that he wanted, and found a ready – though not, I think, always accurate – answer to the questions with which I bombarded him.

His son Jimmy was his assistant, and the eldest of their large family. He was what my father called a 'masher': he coated his hair with pomade, walked with a swagger and ogled the girls. Eventually he seduced 'Truda, which led my mother, who was very prudish at times, instantly to dismiss her, and to his being declared *persona non grata* so far as our household was concerned. Thereupon his duties devolved upon his younger brother, Ernest, a stolid youth and almost as gloomy as his mother.

Augustus Bellborder was well over six feet in height and thin to the point of emaciation. His head was small and quite round; and his deeply sunken eyes, hollow temples and bony brow, his lean, underhung jaw and wide mouth with its big yellow teeth, gave his face the appearance of a skull. The absorbing passion of his life was our drawing-room floor. Other floors he polished well, but this, perhaps because of its numerous fascinating reflections, inspired him. If by some mischance its surface was scratched, he would brood and mutter over it for hours as though he had sustained a personal injury. I can see him now, standing at one end of the room, his hands folded one over the other on top of the broom-stick, his shoulders hunched, his neck thrust forward scraggily from his shirt, his trousers rolled up above his knees displaying his thin shanks, looking for all the world like a battered old marabou stork, as he peered this way and that seeking any filmy patch which might mar the shiny surface and crooning to himself:

' 'E be good? . . . I t'ink 'e be good . . . All de 'flections be plain-plain to see? . . . I t'ink so . . . yes, I t'ink so . . .' And at last: 'Praise de Lord! 'E be well good!'

Augustus scorned all manufactured polishes and concocted a mixture of his own: a task which was conducted with the solemnity of a ritual. He would fill a brazier with charcoal, insert some dry twigs, apply a match, and after a few moments of vigorous blowing, during which the sprays of saliva he ejected seemed to have no damping effect, the coals would be glowing. He had previously sliced a quantity of flakes from a lump of dark wax taken from a wild bees' nest, which, with a piece of Naples soap, was put into a smoke-blackened tin and set upon the fire to melt. Boiled rain-water and turpentine were added. Squatting on his haunches Augustus stirred his mixture with a long stick. Rhythmically, leisurely, round and round he stirred, chanting the while a doleful threnody about his and his family's trials and tribulations, each verse ending with the same refrain:

De Lo-o-ord kin save me, an' de Lo-o-ord kin take me:
Save me or take den, O Lo-o-ord!

When the polish was as smooth as cream Augustus poured it into a large stone jar which, together with the polishing broom and various cloths, was kept in a cupboard in the pantry – and woe betide anyone else who touched these things! If he so much as suspected that someone had so much as opened the door of his cupboard he would become convulsed with rage, and with long arms threshing he would furiously demand:

'Who be dat wut'less pusson what trouble me t'ings? I is askin' yo'-all: who be dis sinful pusson? . . . Let me eyes see dem, let me ears hear dem, let me han's hold dem, an' dey will larn what I kin do!'

But unfortunately for Augustus Bellborder, everyone to whom these words were addressed knew that he would never have hurt a fly!

Lizzie Waldron had been my grandmother's maid at Piedmont. A strange mulatto woman, holding herself aloof from everyone – it was said that her father had been a 'gentleman of consequence' – there was something sinister about her. She received no pension, for she was in need of none, and it was commonly believed that she had robbed my grandmother systematically. A story was told that my grandmother had entrusted to her certain articles of jewellery to pack in a box and take to the Bank for safe keeping. These consisted of a diamond tiara, earrings and bracelets which comprised a set that had been given my grandmother by her father as a wedding gift. After my grandmother's death my grandfather claimed the box. The seals were still intact, but it was found on opening it that all the larger stones had been prised from their settings. There was no evidence really against Lizzie, but it was felt odd that upon retirement she had been able to buy a plot of land in Port-of-Spain and build a comfortable bungalow upon it, where she lived for the remainder of her life with a girl to wait upon her and a man to cultivate her garden.

Her manner was both unctuous and supercilious; her mouth bitter, and her eyes shifty and liver-coloured in a narrow face. She never entered by the back gate, as did all the other old retainers, but always by way of the front, then round the side of the house and so to the back verandah, her whole demeanour contriving to convey that to go to the back verandah at all was an act of condescension on her part which happened to suit her convenience. All this irritated my father, but my mother invariably made excuses for Lizzie, pleading that his mother had allowed such privileges and that she was too old to change her ways. Furthermore, my mother was, in fact, under frequent obligations to her as I shall show in due course.

CHAPTER FIVE

Mary Hodge

Mary Hodge was our laundress. She had been born and brought up at Piedmont and now dwelt in a neat little pink-painted bungalow, about half a mile from our house, with Thorpe – a pleasant young negro whom my English grandmother Amelia had first employed fifty years before when she and my grandfather had first come to Trinidad, and whose duty it had then been to attend upon her whenever she rode forth on her white mule. He had remained in her service until her death and, unlike some of her other servants, had been scrupulously honest, although he had had every opportunity to be otherwise, for she loathed handling money and would entrust him with considerable sums out of which he paid current expenses and of which she never required an account. He could, therefore, have feathered his nest lavishly, but when he finally retired from service to spend his old age in Port-of-Spain he had, with the legacy left him by my grandmother and his own savings, just enough to buy the little pink bungalow and live there in modest comfort. He possessed various trophies of his long service, but these had all been given him by my grandmother because she had grown tired of them herself or wished to replace them with others that had caught her wayward fancy. Of these the principal was a really beautiful mahogany four-poster bed, whose tapering posts were crowned with carved pineapple terminals, of which Thorpe was immensely, and rightly, proud.

I have said that Mary Hodge 'dwelt' with Thorpe, for to say that she 'lived' with him might be misleading. They were certainly not married, yet my mother, who was scandalised by illicit relationships, accepted the fact that these two lived under the same roof with complete equanimity, nor did she seek, so far as I know, to enforce marriage upon them as she did in other instances.

If I were loitering near the gate on a Monday morning I would see Mary coming towards our house along Tranquillity Avenue followed a few paces in the rear by her 'porter' – an emaciated coolie carrying a tray, and hobbling along with the aid of a stick, naked save for a tattered loincloth, with legs so thin that they seemed in danger of snapping in two, with ribs that stuck out so prominently that I automatically counted them with a sickly fascination, and with calluses on his knees and elbows that looked like patches of cow-horn grafted on to his dry scaly skin. While Mary, with a jangle of silver bangles and a rustling of starched petticoats, made her way to the back verandah, the coolie squatted in the shade and immediately fell asleep.

Mary's dresses were whiter than any garments I have ever beheld and so stiffly starched that I believe they could have stood up without her inside them; so perfectly were they ironed that their gloss was dazzling in the sunlight. Against her ebony skin her coral necklace took on a peculiarly rich tone, as did the bright gold of her long earrings. She wore elastic-sided boots of which she was inordinately proud, but they contrived to rob her gait of its natural grace by reason of the fact that they were a size too small for her. She only wore them when she came to our house, and the torture they inflicted was reflected in the strained tautness of her expression and in sundry mutterings and smothered moans, all of which so distressed my mother that she bought Mary another pair that were a proper fit. But though Mary accepted this gift with loud exclamations of gratitude, she kept them carefully preserved in the tissue paper and shiny white box in which they had been bought, and explaining that 'dey be too gran' to spile wid touchin' de ground', continued to hobble, mutter and moan in her misfits in spite of my mother's protests.

After an elaborate exchange of compliments between Mary and my mother, there followed the 'reck'nin' ' of the soiled linen. Chatting and bustling Mary emptied out the baskets

and sorted their contents into piles, then she handed the
laundry book to my mother and proceeded to 'call out de
clo'es'.

'Seven shirts fo' de master. Ten shirts fo' Mistah Gareth . . .
E-e-eh! Look, Madam, I beg yo' see! Dis ev'nin' weskit o'
Mistah Gareth have a burn fo' de front! Mus'-be he do dat wid
a cig'rette. Like it be done spile – look at dat now! . . . See
here, Miss Baby done tear dis good dress – mus'-be clim'in'
trees she do dat . . . Darlin', dat not be right fo' yo' to do.'

The reckoning concluded, Mary spread a sheet on the floor
and began sorting the various articles into 'pieces'. Large
articles, like sheets, each constituted a 'piece', but where the
smaller ones were concerned a certain number composed a
single 'piece'. The term was an elastic one and much was left
to Mary's judgement. The standard charge for each 'piece'
was four cents. There were always a few oddments left over
that fitted in nowhere and these Mary heaped together saying:

'Mus'-be 'bout two pieces an' a li'l lagniappe besides.'

A 'lagniappe' was anything over the standard measure or
weight which was bestowed without charge.

My mother with the aid of her short fingers would now add
up the number of pieces and convert them into terms of
dollars and cents. Being no mathematician she invariably got
confused.

'What does that come to? . . . Six dozen and four pieces at
four cents – these wretched cents! . . . Oh dear! where was I?
. . . Six dozen and four over . . . Is that seventy-six by four, or
forty-eight cents six times? . . . Well, forty-eight cents is two
shillings . . . There! I think that's right.'

Mary meanwhile, apparently indifferent to these tortured
calculations, was tying the opposite corners of the sheet
together, shaking and pulling alternately to get the washing
into a compact bundle. The coolie was roused from his slum-
bers, the bundle lifted on to his head, and as he tottered under
its weight my mother would be sure to exclaim:

'Oh that poor creature! Mary, I'm sure he can't carry that
weight! He looks utterly starved! . . . Here . . . you! – girl! . . .
you! . . . one of you servants!' (In emergencies or moments of
stress my mother invariably forgot everyone's name) '. . . get

a loaf of bread, *quickly*, cut it in half and butter it – put plenty of brown sugar on it, too – and give it to that coolie . . .'

The coolie must have known full well that each Monday morning this scene would be enacted, yet each time the loaf was handed to him his face lit up with surprise and delight, and his hand went to his forehead in a succession of grateful salaams. Then his hunger would overcome all else and as he moved off at a shambling trot with one hand steadying the bundle, with the other he held the loaf to his mouth and tore at it ravenously. He earned sixpence from Mary for this trip, and another sixpence when he brought the laundry back on Friday. God only knew if he earned any more.

How little thought we gave to such poor creatures in those days! Yet there were scores like him – and there are to this day in many countries. Homeless, they slept under a tree or on a public bench. Unemployed, they were thankful to earn a couple of cents carrying a load for an able-bodied negro, who bullied and derided them, and not infrequently cheated them out of even this pittance. Often they were found dead where they had scavenged, at the gutter's edge.

Mary was not only our laundress, she was 'one of us'. In sickness or at any other time when our household needed additional help she would 'drop what she was doin' ' in order to assist. Every line of her face expressed patience and kindliness. I never saw her angry and never heard her give voice to an envious or unkind sentiment.

I ran in and out of the pink bungalow with the same familiar assurance as I ran in and out of my own home. Throughout the first eight years of my life, at which time Mary died, it drew me as a magnet draws a needle, for in the atmosphere of tranquil activity which prevailed there, in Mary's personality and in that of old Thorpe, there was a fundamental wisdom and serenity which ministered to and soothed some indefinable longing in myself. Neither of them could read or write, but then wisdom and knowledge are very different things. A man can easily know many things without being wise – wisdom comes only from 'walking with God'.

Simply to watch Mary at work was to feel a sense of security and timelessness: a guarantee of the essential goodness of humanity. Her yard provided ample evidence of her occupation. There were two huge wash-tubs and a water-tap islanded upon a square of cement paving. There was a pile of fair-sized boulders upon which she 'beat' the washing, a low cement platform upon which she bleached it in the sun, and a row of bamboo poles between which ran the drying line. The rest of the yard was gravelled, save for one corner where there was a cultivated patch with half a dozen shrubs of aubergine, a couple of pepper bushes and a bed of herbs.

The perfection of Mary's laundering was attained by soap, water, sunlight and painstaking labour performed with pride. With the rising of the sun the washing went into the big tubs. There it lay soaking until the afternoon, when Mary took the wooden scrubbing board, whitened with years of use, and girding up her skirts, tackled the contents of the first tub. With a bar of mottled blue and white soap in her hand she copiously lathered each article and rubbed and pounded it on the board between her fists with a crisply squelching sound. Her bare arms became white with soapsuds; iridescent bubbles formed, burst and reformed; and on the scrubbing would go while the sun shone down, and Mary, responding to the rhythm of her toil broke into the strains of a favourite hymn, such as *All Things Bright and Beautiful*.

The clothes were next lifted out of the tub and carried to the heap of boulders, which Mary had sluiced down in readiness. Here, with soapsuds flying in all directions, flecking her face and clinging to the short, tight plaits of her kinky hair, she would whirl one garment after another in the air and bring it down with a loud smack upon the boulders; then bundling all together, she cast them down upon a slatted platform in a shed while she dealt with another tubful.

The following morning all were put out to bleach in the sun. The bleaching would be complete by the afternoon, when they were rinsed under the tap in the yard. The tubs were then made ready for the blueing process, and into them each piece in turn was plunged, squeezed out, then hung on the line to drip.

Mary obtained her 'fine starch' from a *marchande* who made it herself, and if there was the minutest speck of a foreign body in its powdery purity she would indignantly return it to the vendor.

'Take back dis trash, woman. Yo' t'ink I'se gwine put dat in me white-people clo'es?'

With apologies the offender would open another bag, and perhaps several more, before Mary was satisfied that she was obtaining the best.

But most of all I enjoyed the ironing days, when braziers with beds of fiery charcoal were set up on the verandah and a stout white-pine ironing table was spread with blankets under a linen cloth. The lovely smell of the hot iron on the clean starched material, the clank it made each time Mary put it down on the metal triangle over the fire to reheat, the regular rhythmic thumps she made with it on the table as she worked, contrived to create that feeling of continuity, that sense of the old, established simple things which, in a fevered world, form the one root of sanity, are the basis of all contentment, and for which, whether we know it or not, we are continually yearning. So Mary sang and thudded and tended the braziers, her bare feet pattering on the floor, the fragrant steam filling the air, the pile of glossy linen mounting ever higher. Then the big wooden tray, white from continual scrubbing, was spread with a square of muslin, and first the household linen and then the clothing were laid upon it. The smaller articles were tucked in a basket with a loop handle, and each Friday morning this was 'toted' back to our house by Mary herself, as she hobbled in her tight boots a pace or two ahead of her tottering porter, under the heavy tray.

In the midst of Mary's bustling activities Thorpe lived a life of total leisure. He usually wore a pair of baggy old trousers and a collarless shirt, and swung in a bentwood rocking chair as he gossiped with such cronies as came his way. But on Sundays his attire was elaborate. Then he would don a frock coat, rather green with age but kept by Mary pressed and speckless, and a pair of blue serge trousers of a more recent date which had once been my father's. A starched collar of Gladstonian pattern was encircled by a pink piqué tie which passed through an embossed silver ring, and on his feet were white cotton socks and black, elastic-sided boots.

At four o'clock on the first Sunday of every month, dressed in this resplendence, he would call on my father. Ushered into the study he held his stove-pipe hat – one of the greatest of his treasures – upon his knee as he sat very rigid and upright in the chair my father offered him. They talked of all manner of things, from local happenings to the stars, and from the stars to days of yore. The visit lasted about an hour and then Thorpe took his leave, wending his way past the servants' quarters, bowing ceremoniously to everyone he met, his hat set at a jaunty angle, and a cigar, my father's invariable gift, flourished conspicuously between the fingers of his right hand, to be retained for smoking that evening among his circle of cronies while he repeated all that my father had said with the impressive solemnity of one who had visited an oracle.

Thorpe's death was sudden. One evening there came a message from Mary to say that he had been taken ill: that she had sent for the doctor, and that the doctor had sent medicine. My mother set out for the bungalow with 'Truda in her wake carrying a basket of delicacies – including a cigar – but Thorpe was already past the enjoyment of earthly delights, and at dawn he died. A shadow lay athwart our house. It pressed down upon me, stupefyingly.

Thorpe was dead . . . Death! . . . I had seen dead birds and animals, and frequently had heard that someone or other 'was dead'. But what did it really mean? I had seen any number of funerals going past our house from All Saints Church to the cemetery at the bottom of Tranquillity Avenue. Through the glass panels of the hearses I had seen the coffins, highly polished, bound in brass and heaped with flowers. I had watched the slow sad processions of the mourners and heard the solemn tolling of the bell. But hitherto the fact of death had made small impression upon me.

Now with the death of Thorpe – someone I had known intimately – death for the first time touched me closely. It seemed incredible that he would never come to our house again; that when I ran into the pink bungalow his bentwood rocker would be empty; that never again should I see his mild, benevolent countenance or hear his slow, rather husky voice. As I thought of these things a lump came into my throat and tears stung my eyes, while a passionate curiosity as to death assailed me. What did Thorpe look like now? His soul, pre-

sumably was in Heaven – but his body . . .? I had heard the
negroes say: 'When yo' dead yo' caint take nuttin wid yo'!' So
would Thorpe then have to leave behind even his frock coat
and the tall hat which he loved so much . . .? Were the dead,
then, buried . . . *naked* . . .? I asked Estelle. She was shocked
and horrified.

'But how yo' ask dat, chil'? Shame 'pon you'! Bury people
naked! I nebber hear sich a t'ing!'

'But what happens then?'

'Dey does put dey bes' clo'es 'pon dem. Dat does be
respec'ful to dem an' to de Lawd. How yo' want people to sen'
dey dead naked to de Lawd? E-e-eh! No matter how poo' a
pusson is dey will dress-up dey dead. Only pussons dat have
no family *at-all at-all* dey does wrap up in a sheet, an' gib
pauper burial to.'

I pondered this information with relief, for Mary would see
that Thorpe took his best suit with him. And the tall hat? My
curiosity was stirred to a fever which urged me to go to the
bungalow and see for myself. I *must* find out; I must find out
all sorts of things . . . I felt that I was on the threshold of some
great discovery; that the solution of some ancient mystery lay
within my grasp. Yet fear – fear of the unknown, fear of things
unearthly – made me shrink back.

In the end curiosity won. I crept out of the gate and stole
along Tranquillity Avenue towards the bungalow, my heart
pounding, feeling at once guilty and daring, knowing that my
mother would be shocked and angry if she knew what I was
doing; terrified of what I might see, yet drawn irresistibly
on . . .

The gate yielded to my touch. I stole up the steps, through
the front door, closing it soundlessly behind me. I crossed the
familiar little parlour with its coloured plates of sacred subjects on its walls. My eyes flew to the empty bentwood rocker,
and to the oval table next to it with its marble top draped with
a crochet cloth on which lay the large, worn Bible I had so
often seen in old Thorpe's hands as he pretended to read, his
lips repeating passages firmly fixed in youth. Each object in
that room – strangely, heavily silent now – possessed a sudden piercingly new significance.

Feeling sick and empty I laid my fingers on the handle of the door into Thorpe's room. Trembling, my teeth close to chattering, I turned it and opened the door just sufficiently to squeeze my body through. There, clinging to it for support, I stood.

The windows of the room were closed, which made it dim, but enough light filtered in between the jalousies to show me a rigid form upon the four-poster under a snow white sheet. I stared at it wavering between fascination and panic. The atmosphere was heavy with a smell like camphor – and something else which I could not name but which seemed to hold me by the throat. A sudden awful dread seized me that the rigid form would sit up, grim and accusing, utterly changed from the Thorpe I had known, and upbraid me for my temerity . . . I longed to slide out; to shut the door between it and me and run away, I bitterly regretted coming – yet I could not go; could not drag my eyes away from the form on the bed. Dimly I grew aware of the ticking of a clock, while outside some chicks were cheeping and a mother hen clucking to them encouragingly. These sounds, so familiar and normal, gave me a certain relief. I edged into the room and took a step towards the bed. There I came to a halt. I could go no further. Still less dare I contemplate lifting the sheet to look at what lay beneath.

Ages seemed to pass while I stood as though hypnotised, my hands locked painfully together. Then I heard the shuffle of slippered feet and Mary was beside me.

'Miss Baby!' she gasped in a startled whisper, 'How come yo' here-so?'

'I . . . I . . . came to see Thorpe,' I quavered.

'Yo' nebber know Mistah T'orpe be dead?'

'Yes . . . I . . . I knew . . . but I came to see him . . . I wanted to see him.' I clasped her hand, swallowing at the lump in my throat and trying to swallow my dread with it. 'Let me see him, Mary.'

Mary hesitated.

'Mebbe yo' mudder would be vex' . . .'

'I won't tell her . . . I want to see Thorpe . . .'

She led me to the bed without more ado and lifted the sheet. There lay Thorpe, his eyes closed, his face set into a bland, smooth remoteness which made a stranger of him.

So many questions seethed in my overcharged mind, swelling and shrinking with the thudding of my heart and the hammering of my pulses; why was his skin that strange colour – the weathered and silvery colour of ancient wood? What was that other smell beside the camphor – that stuffy, sickly-sweet smell?

He lay dressed in the clothes he wore to call upon my father, even to the white socks and the elastic-sided boots. The tall hat stood beside him, and the points of the stiff collar were piercing the immobile chin.

'I put all he good-clo'es 'pon he,' Mary was whispering, her voice strangled with emotion. 'So he wished fo' me to do.' Her clasp on my hand tightened. 'He mus' be glad to t'ink yo' come an' see he . . . He done gone to de Lawd.' Then she bowed her head and wept.

My whole body felt as rigid as Thorpe's. Mary's grief broke the frail courage I had won, and overwhelmed me. A wave of nausea and sadness swept over me. Tearing my hand from hers I fled blindly out of that twilit gloom into the dazzling sunshine.

After Thorpe's death Mary took an elderly coloured woman to live with her – to 'make comp'ny fo' me,' she explained. This woman effaced herself so effectively that I never knew her name. With Thorpe no longer alive to claim her attention Mary's visits on Mondays and Fridays grew more protracted, and she took to 'lookin' in' on other days of the week as well. We were her only link with all she had loved and all that had made up her entire life. Then one day, some two years later, she arrived with a bandaged forefinger and the hand itself puffy and swollen. A pin, she told us, had gone in under the nail and the place had festered.

'You should see the doctor at the hospital about it at once,' my mother urged. 'It doesn't do to neglect a thing like that.'

'E-e-h Madam? How yo' want I go bodderin' de doctor wid a li'l t'ing like dis? De doctor would rightly race me out de place fo' dat! It gwine come better soon-soon, please Gawd.'

But next day she called to tell us that she was on her way to the hospital, adding:

'Me han' give me a set o' bodderation. Las' night I get no

res' at-all-at-all. De pain passin' me elbow an' reachin, mos' to me breast.'

Her face was drawn and pinched; her voice was flat and expressionless and she was strangely altered. I remember tightly clasping the post at the foot of the verandah steps, feeling suddenly frightened and despairing. With some instinct I knew that death was upon her.

My mother was very upset. She ordered a cab to be called and bade 'Truda accompany Mary to the hospital. I watched them drive away together in the ramshackle conveyance, the hooves of the starved old horse beating upon the hard, white surface of the road in a doom-burdened monotone. I knew I should never see Mary again, and as they passed out of sight I went with lagging steps to the saman to brood in swamping, uncomprehending grief.

In a matter of hours it was all over. There was an emergency amputation, and Mary did not survive.

CHAPTER SIX

My Grandfather's Story

My grandfather, Robert Guppy, was disappointed that my father had shown no inclination towards the law, for he would have liked a son of his to have inherited his large, interesting and lucrative practice; but I think he had come to realise that the legal profession was foreign to my father's temperament, and that his scientific studies completely absorbed him. Nevertheless he refused to take a partner, arguing that if there was no son to succeed him it did not matter what became of the practice after he himself was dead.

Although now a widower, he still lived in some style, dressing for dinner every night even when he was alone – which was regarded locally as a somewhat eccentric proceeding – and sitting down to a table as carefully appointed as when he entertained, which he did frequently.

'Remember your grandfather is an old gentleman: you must do nothing to fatigue him – he is not used to children,' we were told, ignoring the fact that he had had four of his own.

The impetus that had driven my grandfather to Trinidad came originally from that convulsive period of wars and revolutions at the end of the 18th and beginning of the 19th centuries when the rights of man were first proclaimed and the modern world first began to take shape. For the Guppys those times brought immediate good fortune. For centuries they had lived in western Dorset within a few miles of the lost village of Guppy, still marked on the map but now uninhabited, a maze of crumbling walls and mounds on a hillside over-looking the sea. Then calamine, important in the making of copper, a crucial industrial material, was discovered on some family property, and my great-grandfather Samuel Guppy had moved to Bristol and set himself up as a copper merchant, iron-founder and West India merchant. He and his wife Sarah were highly inventive, and before long between them had devised one of Britain's secret weapons of the Napoleonic Wars: so important that the British Government purchased the rights of manufacture for £40,000 – a huge sum in those days. This device was called 'the patent sheathing nail', and it enabled copper to be fastened to the bottoms of wooden ships with greater ease than hitherto, and set up also a very mild electrolytic action which inhibited the growth of barnacles. As a result the British fleet could stay at sea longer than the French, and could sail faster. The Patent Sheathing Nail Manufactory issued an abundance of 1d and $\frac{1}{2}$d tokens in 1811 and 1812, and these can commonly be found at coin merchants to this day.

Samuel Guppy's oldest son had married the daughter of Philip Protheroe, whose family had purchased estates in Trinidad soon after it was captured by the British in 1797; and my grandfather Robert, his youngest son, was soon handling some of the Protheroe's legal problems. He had graduated from Pembroke College, Oxford, had been called to the Bar of the Middle Temple, and in 1834, the year that slavery was abolished in Trinidad, had married Amelia Parkinson, of Kinnersley Castle, Herefordshire. She was a lady of wildly independent mould and adventurous spirit, as well as of considerable talent as an artist. She had fallen in love with my grandfather as tempestuously as she did most things, and although the marriage was approved by the parents on both sides, they had forestalled it by eloping secretly: he whisked her away by carriage one dark night to the home of her cousins, the Walcots, at Bitterly Court in Shropshire, where they married a few days later.

After their marriage they lived at 35 Chancery Lane, and there my aunt Lucy and my father and my uncle Francis were born.

In 1835 my grandfather published *A Familiar Abridgement of the Municipal Corporation Act* which, together with his work on circuit with the judges rapidly established his reputation as an unusually energetic and promising lawyer. He seemed set for a conventional legal career of some brilliance.

Then Colonel Protheroe had invited him to go to Trinidad and act as his attorney in all matters arising from the Abolition of Slavery. The Portheroe estates were in the south of the island, and in the course of his visit my grandfather had met and struck up a warm friendship with Leon Toussaint Rostant, head of the Rostant family, who was known as 'The King of Couva' from the style in which he lived on his principal estate.

He had also visited the valley of Diego Martin, where some dozen miles from the capital, Port-of-Spain, there happened to be two estates for sale known as Diamond and Endeavour. On his return to England his descriptions of them, of their luxuriant fertility, of the hills that enfolded them, of the pellucid stream that babbled through them, of the rare orchids that grew there, and the exotic birds and butterflies, made such an instant appeal to his wife's impulsive enthusiasm and love of beauty and adventure that they lost no time in purchasing the estates and making known their resolve to settle in Trinidad.

Their relatives and friends were appalled! They protested that such a step would mean the jettisoning of my grandfather's career. They pointed out that there were three young children to be considered, and that the young couple would be cutting themselves off from everyone they knew. They pointed out that wiser folk were foretelling that the end of slavery would be the downfall and ruin of the plantation system; but my grandfather was an optimist where all others were pessimists: he believed in freedom and the natural energy of men. He and his wife ignored all warnings. The house in Chancery Lane was sold; two of the children, Francis and Lucy, were despatched to their grandparents at Clifton; my father, Lechmere, to live with his maternal grandfather at Kinnersley; while they themselves, accompanied by innumerable crates containing their furniture, silver, linen and other household effects, and by enormous trunks of clothes, set sail.

They arrived at the best season of the year. The vegetation

was lush and verdant after the recent rains, the air cool and delicious. My grandfather's previous mission to the island had already won him recognition and they received a cordial welcome.

My grandmother bought a white mule and a chestnut pony: the former for herself to ride, the latter for Thorpe, then a young man, whom she engaged as her personal attendant, and followed by whom, weighted down with her artistic paraphernalia, she explored the surrounding countryside. Where she elected to sketch he would set up her easel, and stand behind the stool on which she sat, holding a vast green-lined parasol over her head. This young man was Thorpe, whose death I have recounted in the last chapter.

My grandmother soon began to form a collection of orchids which she induced to grow in the trees about their house. She made paintings of them, classified and named them, as she did innumerable other plants. But, unfortunately, her activities did not end there, She also developed extravagant plans for improving the property. She decided to rebuild the plantation house using the most beautiful native woods, and to surround it with a park-like pleasance, to enclose which she ordered from England an elaborate wrought-iron fence.

It was many months before the fence arrived, and when it did it lay on the quay at Port-of-Spain for an equally long time: for in the interval the rains had broken and with their advent the pellucid, babbling stream had become an angry torrent which tore up trees and swept away bridges, while the road to Port-of-Spain became an impassable quagmire. Daily the clouds banked upon the hills making the heat in the valley as steamy and insufferable as that of a hot-house, while the mosquitos and sandflies descended in swarms to feast on her delicate skin.

But there was worse to come. My grandfather was making a number of unpleasant discoveries. One was that he had paid, in his hasty purchase of the properties, a fantastically high price for them; another, that his manager and overseers were systematically robbing him. He was learning the hard way that the successful ownership of a plantation required knowledge and experience. So while the iron fence lay on the quay in Port-of-Spain my grandparents were becoming as disillusioned a young couple as ever stared failure in the face. They had spent money prodigally, fondly assuring themselves that their crops would compensate for their expenditure. But the crops proved poor in quality and much depleted by theft. So work on house and pleasance were abandoned, and by the time the innumerable sections of the wrought-iron fence had at last been laboriously conveyed to the estate, they were left to rust where they lay* for everything was already up for sale to liquidate as many debts as possible.

Before leaving for England my grandparents revisited the south of the island where, staying with Leon Toussaint Rostant's son Leonard at La Coulée, near San Fernando, a new idea entered my grandfather's mind. Half a mile from La Coulée, and on the same steep hillside, was a similar house called La Falaise, and below it, connected by a bridge across a deep ravine, there stood a smaller house called Piedmont. These were Rostant properties, named not only because of the appropriateness of their situation ('The Cliff' and 'Hill Foot' in English) but after the homes of distinguished ancestors – William the Conqueror and the Princes of Piedmont! San Fernando was a rapidly growing town, second only to Port-of-Spain itself, and the centre of a thriving agricultural district. And the Rostants had just put all this portion of the hillside up for sale. My grandparents discussed the matter and decided that they had had enough of valleys and more than enough of estate ownership; that he was a lawyer by profession and not a planter; but that despite their recent experiences they still loved Trinidad. Before long they had bought the hillside. At first they furnished La Falaise as their home and Piedmont as an office, though later they moved into Piedmont and kept La Falaise for guests. Then my grandfather set himself up as a practising lawyer once again. In a very short time he had become a remarkably successful one.

He made a niche for himself that exactly suited him, and I am sure he never regretted the more brilliant career that he

---

* When some hundred years later, I last visited Endeavour Estate (which had become by that time a Government experimental plantation) I saw sections of that famous fence being used to support pumpkin vines in the gardens of neighbouring negro shanties.

might have had in England, for he came to hold a unique position in Trinidad and to be regarded as a unique personality. His mode of life was dignified, and his days were charged with a variety of interests. He was a magistrate and was re-elected mayor of San Fernando year after year. He was frequently consulted both by the Foreign Office and the local government on various questions of policy, and was for many years a member of the Legislative Council.

I do not know what my grandmother's more considered reactions to all this were, and I can hardly believe that they were favourable for long. For neither her temperament nor her upbringing fitted her for life in Trinidad. On the estates her creative instincts had at least found a temporary outlet, and she had shared with her husband a mutual interest and occupation. But at San Fernando she could take no part in his professional activities and, apart from her painting, there was little to capture her mind or imagination. She missed the intellectual and artistic stimulus of the circles in which she had moved in England, and found her society restricted to that of people whose interests and outlook were severely limited. Their narrow preoccupations were as wearisome to her as the scope of her intelligence was intimidating to them. She found them boring and tedious, and they found her incomprehensible and alarming.

When my grandparents had settled into La Falaise they had begun, naturally, to improve the place. They had made a winding drive down the hillside and a terraced garden for which they imported rose trees from England, and fruit and flowering trees from other tropical lands. They had made an aviary and a small 'zoo'. But once this was all completed her art was the only solace for her growing sense of frustration, and she took to wandering ever further afield in search of fresh subjects.

For miles around San Fernando she became a familiar figure, mounted on her white mule, clad in her riding-habit with its tight-fitting jacket and long flowing skirt, a wide-brimmed hat upon her head, a floating veil about her face, a jabot of lace at her throat and yellow gauntlets upon her hands; attended always by the faithful Thorpe astride the pony, carrying the painting equipment and the green-lined parasol. There was something remote and exotic in her appearance, yet every-thing also of the *grande dame*. As they watched her ride past people were bewildered: they could not understand how anyone so elegant could wish to traverse miles of country under the blazing sun in order to make a few sketches, or risk fever and snake-bite searching for flowers in a swamp, instead of relaxing into the genteel indolence proper to a lady.

Whenever her longing for her children and the life she had abandoned grew unendurable, my grandmother would hurry to England, but her love for my grandfather always drew her back to Trinidad. This ceaseless tug-of-war between heart and brain tormented her and gave her no peace. Neither with my grandfather nor without him could she find con-tentment. And this of course affected her children, particu-larly my father, as I have related.

Perhaps the climax of her life was when at the age of sixty-three, in 1871, she conceived the notion of exploring the upper reaches of the Orinoco river in Venezuela, into which no white man, let alone woman, had ever ventured for any distance – indeed the source of this mighty river was only discovered in 1951. Its rapids were phenomenally dangerous, its jungles dense, forbidding and fever ridden, and its native Indians were notoriously savage and unpredictable in behaviour. Today the mere thought of a woman embarking alone on such an expedition would engage the shrillest atten-tion of all the organs of publicity. A century ago these had not yet attained their present ubiquity, so my grandmother's solitary expedition passed unnoticed outside the island of Trinidad. But there it created no small sensation, and there was much horrified head-shaking and wonderment as to her sanity. But undeterred by protests and warnings, she went – and contrary to every expectation, she returned.

But the expedition was not without its tragic consequence. She was gone for over a year, during which no news of her reached her family. Finally my uncle Francis set off up the Orinoco river to seek her. Their canoes passed each other in the night unknowingly, he going up river, she returning. Just as she reached home safely, and in good health, he contracted a malignant fever and died, in the prime of his manhood.

She died in 1886, two years before I was born, an old

woman burned out by her own flame. She left no record of her Orinoco adventures other than a series of floral studies and a collection of orchids, some of which were still flourishing under an arbour at Piedmont long after her death. Even sixty years later her beauty, her distinction and her exploits were still legendary in Trinidad: the 'mad Mrs Guppy' who lived in the jungle in a tree house; while even outside the island there were those who remembered her. Before the Second World War I met an old lady living in Sussex who had known her in her last years, and who told me of her wasted genius, and of the despairing expression of her eyes, so forlorn that they had continued to haunt her.

CHAPTER SEVEN

Visiting Piedmont

—◦❦◦—

In spite of misgivings as to the embarrassments into which our behaviour might plunge her, my mother looked forward to her visits to Piedmont tremendously. She revelled in the air of elegance that prevailed, and in my grandfather's ceremonious way of life. She revelled in the sense of prestige which acting as his hostess gave her; and, sitting at the foot of the long table with its festive array of glittering crystal, shining silver and delicate porcelain, she was in her element. She loved the mellow old furniture, and she would say that simply to move from room to room among such lovely things made her happy.

For weeks before Christmas she launched a campaign to coax money out of my father – who 'listened groaning, and groaning gave' – to provide herself and us with the additional clothes which her vanity persuaded her were necessary. She was well aware that my grandfather found her fascinating, and she spared no pains to impress and charm him, and a compliment from him stimulated her like wine. So fashion papers surrounded her, dressmakers were closeted with her, and as messengers hurried to and from the shops with patterns of materials, ribbons and laces for her to choose from, friends whose taste she valued gathered round to advise and admire as she made her selections or stood before her cheval mirror being fitted. If my father called a halt to further expenditure before her desires were satisfied, or if Ruth came to her with the plea that she needed another frock or pair of shoes, a distracted look would come into my mother's eyes.

'Yes, dear, I know; but your father says he can't afford anything more. I must *think* . . . *Somehow* or other you shall have what you want.'

Then with many sighs and puckerings of the brow she would decide upon the desperate expedient of selling a piece of jewellery or silver. And this was the obligation under which she lay to Lizzie Waldron, for my mother employed Lizzie to negotiate the actual disposal of the articles.

A shadow would cloud my mother's face while one of these transactions was in progress, for her natural honesty disdained subterfuge. But with her, the need of the moment was all imperative, and her face would lighten as the various spinstresses who had been sent to purchase required things returned with them smuggled under their skirts or concealed in the folds of their parasols. But what if my father should miss the object which had been sold to provide them? He might not; or if he did it might be long enough hence for her almost to have forgotten the incident and the discovery of the loss would evoke a dismay which was nearly genuine. Otherwise she relied upon eventual confession and a show of abject penitence to disarm my father's anger, which it invariably did.

My father enjoyed the visits to Piedmont no less than my mother, but for different reasons. He was immensely interested in the geology of the southern part of the island, and had come to the conclusion that petroleum existed there long before that belief was put to the test and proved. There were also Carib settlements to be excavated, and their flints and pottery to be discovered. Nearby were sea beaches along which he would wade, casting his net for marine specimens, and places where a slice of subsoil, washed and drained, would yield a rich harvest of *foraminifera*. Indoors there was his father's extensive library in which to browse, and though he would never have admitted it, he too enjoyed the ease and comfort of Piedmont and the stimulating influence of meeting new people and renewing old acquaintanceships at his father's parties. Although he and my grandfather were temperamentally the opposite of each other, they were linked by mutual affection and respect. They might, and did, differ on a host of subjects and get close to acrimony in their arguments, but each valued the opinion of the other no less highly for that.

There were indeed two things which united them at all times, which were a deep concern for their fellow men, especially the poor and powerless; and a profound sense of justice. My grandfather's impartiality had been established once and for all some forty years before, as a young magistrate, when he had sentenced a well-known European lady to forty days in jail for receiving stolen lumber – an action which had caused a sensation. Slavery had been abolished in 1834 and in the years that followed his arrival in the Colony he had fought to get the Crown to release land in smallholdings for settlement by the freed, which he felt was important in developing and diversifying the island for the benefit of all. He had become known as a champion of poor men's rights, and had been strongly opposed by the majority of sugar planters, who feared that they would lose their workers if freed slaves could obtain farms of their own.

My French great-grandfather, Leon Toussaint Rostant, had been a master with whom most of his former slaves had opted to stay, and indeed many more came to him from other plantations. But some planters lost their entire labour force, and there was a general shortage of workers. Leon Toussaint, a powerful member of the Legislative Council, was one of those who proposed to solve this problem by bringing to Trinidad large numbers of Hindu labourers from over-crowded India, to work for a period of five years, at the end of which time they could choose between repatriation or receiving a freehold grant of land.

My grandfather, despite his friendship with Leon Toussaint, foresaw racial and social disharmony, and that the ordinary citizen in underwriting the sugar planter would also be impoverishing himself. He said 'The chief object of the local legislature is by every conceivable device to force down the price of labour, and to confine it to the cultivation of the sugar cane by importing labour at the public expense to be indentured to plantations, and by taxing the necessary food of the working man.' Seeking an alternative, in 1844 he persuaded the Colonial Government to send him to Sierra Leone in West Africa on the barque *Senator*. Sierra Leone had been established as a home for freed slaves, and his object was to see if he could persuade some of them to go back to the Caribbean. He found many of them unsettled, unhappy and disorganised: but he also found that they had re-established a slave society of their own, so that few of them were free to make decisions for themselves, for fear of their masters. Nonetheless a large number elected to return to Trinidad of their own free will, and did so. The full report was published in an address to the House of Commons in 1848.

This is a little known episode in the history of the Africans in the New World, but it is significant, because it is one of the few cases where we can see through the eyes of the negroes the relative merits of a free choice in which they knew both sides. The horror of slavery as an institution is not to be condoned, but slavery was over (at least in the British territories), and in practice the lives and working conditions of free men and women in those days were often as bad. Here we know that memories did not deter them, and it is pleasant to consider that at least some of the Africans in the Caribbean came freely.

In fact slavery was never severe in Trinidad, for from the time of its conquest the British Government had ruled the island directly, in order to limit the powers of the local planters and to protect the slaves: slaves could own and bequeath property, prosecute their masters for ill-treatment, and buy their own freedom for the small sum of twenty shillings; they could not be set free just because they were too old to work and their masters did not wish to support them, nor could their families be broken up. Memories of slave societies in Africa, and the fact that there were many free black people in Trinidad who owned slaves, prevented the issue becoming a direct matter of one race oppressing another. Black men were members of the Legislative Council in the 19th century and there was never any question of enforced racial segregation. The resultant mildness of inter-racial tension has been a blessing to Trinidad, and it allowed that deep and natural affection between people of different conditions which I have described as existing between our various retainers and ourselves. Today this is not so easy to find, because people no longer accept their born positions in life, or contentedly enjoy 'what God has given them'. They want more, and they get more. But they are the lonelier for it.

My grandfather had become very ill during his trip, so he never returned to Sierra Leone. He was rewarded for his efforts by the gift of a small island, once called Guppy Island (now Little Gasparile), near the entrance to Port-of-Spain harbour, which was eventually re-possessed by the Crown, being of high strategic importance, when my absent-minded father forgot to pay his taxes.

Not enough immigrants had come from Sierra Leone, even my grandfather was forced to admit, so in May 1845 the first Hindu settlers arrived, and they continued to arrive until 1916 and to be repatriated for many years after. With this expanding labour force Leon Toussaint Rostant was able to develop and increase his plantations so successfully that during the years after 1845 he became the greatest single proprietor in the West Indies.

Not all sugar planters were like Leon Toussaint, for while he and his family visited Europe frequently, Trinidad was their home; they lived on their plantations, their management was his prime occupation, and he was deeply concerned with the welfare of his employees. But many absentee or exploitative landlords also existed, and despite legal restraints the conditions of employment and housing of the immigrant workers were often soul-destroying or outright appalling. In his *History of the People of Trinidad and Tobago*, Dr Eric Williams, the first Prime Minister after Independence, quotes my grandfather as saying to a Royal Commission in 1888:

As first in the list of evils which afflict the Colony, I look upon the system of housing the Indian Immigrants in barracks . . . The Barrack is a long wooden building eleven or twelve feet wide, containing perhaps eight or ten small rooms divided from each other by wooden partitions not reaching to the roof. By standing on a box the occupant of one room can look over the partition into the adjoining one, and can easily climb over. A family has a single room in which to bring up their boys and girls if they have children. All noises and talking and smells pass through the open space from one end of the barrack to the other. There are no places for cooking, no latrines. The men and women, boys and girls, go together into the canes or bush when nature requires. Comfort, privacy and decency are impossible. A number of these barracks are grouped together close to the dwelling house of the overseers, in order that they may with the least trouble put them out to work before daylight in crop time, which they do by entering their room and, if necessary, pulling them off their beds where they are lying with their wives. If a man is sick he is not allowed to be nursed by his wife, he must perforce go to the hospital far away, leaving his wife, perhaps without the means of subsistence, to her own devices. With all this, can any one wonder at the frequent wife-murders and general demoralisation amongst the Indian immigrants? In fact the barrack life is one approaching to promiscuous intercourse. And the evil is not confined to the coolies. The owner in England compares notes with other absentees and expects his crop to be made at the lowest rate. As to the means, that matters not to him. The overseer holds his situation subject to twenty-four or forty-eight hours' notice and to escape losing his place and consequent beggary he must have but one object in view: that of screwing the most he can out of his bondsman.

It is forty miles from Port-of-Spain to San Fernando. In these days that distance is covered by car in an hour, but in those the only form of transport consisted of hot and dirty trains which jolted along at a speed which seldom exceeded fifteen miles an hour between stops that were frequent and prolonged, with the result that the journey took the greater part of the day.

These journeys provided one of the occasions when I was thankful not to be grown up. The sticky heat took the curl out of fringes, kept complexions moist, and made powder congeal; noses grew shiny and smuts alighted upon them; dresses got grimy and hands in white kid gloves uncomfortably clammy. Such things as powder compacts lay in the future and the use of powder was anyhow considered of questionable propriety – so the ladies' only means of repairing the ravages of the journey was to carry a dusting of face-powder on a tuft of cotton-wool secreted in their handkerchiefs, with which from time to time they dabbed their faces agitatedly and surreptitiously, as though committing a felony, inquiring of each other in strained whispers:

'Is anyone looking? For goodness sake go on talking as though nothing were happening while I put a little powder on.'

At frequent intervals they would ask one another anxiously:

'Is there a smut on my nose? I'm sure I can see one when I look down . . . Have I any powder creases? . . . Is my fringe appalling? I can feel the perspiration under it! Oh, isn't this heat *suffocating*!'

They were so distracted by these things that they could hardly spare a glance for the canefields and cocoa plantations through which the train was crawling; they had no eyes for the crowded station platforms with their concourses of gesticulating negroes, suave Chinese and tranquil Indians all in finery, or with the women vendors of sweetmeats, cakes and fruit; they became more and more irritable as the heat increased and grabbed fretfully at my clothes to pull me back as I craned excitedly out of the window – and when we drew near the journey's end what a frantic tidying up there was!

'Bite your lips, dear, they are so pale . . . Bend down as though you were doing something to your shoe while I fix your fringe – and give your cheeks a pinch to put a little colour into them.'

Then there would surely be cries of:

'Just look at Baby! Look at the state of her hands! Look how she has creased her sailor suit!'

But the moment the train drew up Estelle would sprint along to our carriage and, producing a towel, a bottle of water, and a comb from a little basket, would begin to make me presentable, protesting the while:

'Chil', de state yo' drawers is in! Why yo' mus' drag yo'self on dem dirty seats? . . . Stay still while I 'range yo'.'

As the buggies which had been sent to meet us jogged along the road there were old landmarks to be recognised and new ones to exclaim at. But as we turned into the drive, and lips were again being bitten and cheeks pinched, I grew subdued. Grandpa would be standing, erect and slender in spite of his years, very perfectly groomed and cool-looking, at the top of the front steps to greet us, with his major-domo, Peters, in his spotless white livery with gilt buttons and scarlet waistcoat, close behind him. Hastily I would wipe my hands on my clothes in case they were moist and tuck a straggle of hair behind the elastic of my sailor hat. Arriving at

Grandpa's was something of an ordeal.

But it was tremendous fun at Piedmont. The zoo and aviary afforded a special interest. The boys went off with butterfly nets, Ruth flitted and danced about the hillside in rapt remoteness, and I had endless distractions of my own. Like my mother I found satisfaction in just roaming through the various rooms. The whole atmosphere of the house was one of tranquillity, ease and restraint: that of our house I likened to a river, but that of Piedmont was a deep, shady pool whose still surface lay smooth and unrippled in windless calm.

Peters saw to it that not a door squeaked on its hinges, that no raucous vulgar laughter or discordant voice disturbed the quietude which brooded over it. Never have I known any tropical house where domestic duties were performed with such silent, unobtrusive efficiency, especially considering the number of servants employed.

'If anything were to happen to Peters . . . !' my mother would say, and the gesture she made expressed more eloquently than words the enormity of such a catastrophe. 'Your grandfather hasn't the least idea what he possesses, what his housekeeping costs, nor even how many servants he employs. Without Peters he would be robbed right and left! But Peters is getting very old: he can't be far short of eighty and he can't keep so sharp a look-out on things as once he could. Sometimes I wonder if the other servants don't steal as it is. I tremble to think what losses may eventually be discovered.'

Time was to justify these fears.

Even Augustus Bellborder could have found little fault with the polished floors at Piedmont, and the patina on the mahogany furniture was perfect. In every room were the most entrancing objects. In the drawing-room there were Dresden china wall-vases, always filled with roses and sprays of ferns. There were Dresden china figurines of shepherds and shepherdesses with flowers painted about their feet and a lamb beside them. Once, I am ashamed to say, I deliberately crumbled the filigree lace on the petticoat of one such figure, just to see what it felt like, but when I saw its beauty dissolve between my fingers I was so overcome with remorse that I fled to the top of the hill to brood on the evil I had done. And once, too, I unpicked some beads from an exquisite beadwork footstool to make a necklace for my doll. There was a crystal chandelier and two silver witchballs pendant from the panel-led ceiling, and these last reflected in miniature and with an arresting brilliance every object in the room and vistas of the garden beyond it. On the writing table was a snow-storm paper-weight and in a glass-topped show-table a collection of patch-boxes and snuff-boxes, of silver, gold and Battersea enamel: there were miniatures on ivory of ancestors, some curious rings, my grandmother's gold thimble, and many other pretty trifles. This little table was kept locked and Peters had the key, but sometimes he would open it for me and let me handle the contents.

The dining-room was long and surrounded by a verandah on three sides, on to which six pairs of doors opened. Be-tween each doorway stood a gilt and marble console, its long mirror reflecting the silver candelabra on the dining table; upon each one of these consoles stood a bowl of flowers, and often the humming birds darted through the doors to them, their colours flashing, and sometimes they attacked their reflections in the mirrors with such violence that they fell to the floor stunned and had to be revived with little drops of brandy and water.

As these mirrors multiplied the sheen and scintillation of glass and silver on the table at dinner time, so they added a festive tone to the whole décor. When a party was in progress I would find a dark corner of the verandah from which I could watch the proceedings unseen. The ladies in their billowing skirts, boned bodices, tiny waists and large puff sleeves, their hair dressed high on their heads and ornamented with osprey plumes or clusters of flowers, their arms encased in long white gloves ('four fingers above the elbow'), all looked so gracious that I longed for the time when I, too, should be grown up and take my place in such a scene as this. Then, too, when I was grown up things would at last be the right size. The dining-room table – oh, wonderful thought! – upon which I could now only rest my chin, would be below my hips. Now I was a perpetual misfit. If I sat back in a chair, my feet stuck out absurdly. At meals I had to be brought up to the right height by a footstool: everything placed me at a disadvantage, while grown-ups were all too prone to be amused and facetious at my expense, against which the armour of my dignity was pitifully thin.

Unlike most small girls I had no desire to change my sex. Boys were tiresome and men wore such dull clothes. No: it was more fun, I decided to be a girl. Besides, I would not have such long years at school and when I was grown up I would be courted. I would flutter my fan and glance up and sideways and down as men talked to me. Then I would marry and my husband would make money which I could spend on frocks and cakes and sweets and tins of Combies . . . So I thought as I looked on at the ladies flirting their fans, the men twirling their moustaches, or inclining towards each other. Such lovely *bon-bons* were in little silver dishes; the white-clad servants with their bright waist-coats moved so soundlessly; there was such a hum of voices, of laughter.

On the back verandah at Piedmont, as at most of the big houses in the country at that date, there stood a long table with a bench on either side. It was unpolished, but well scrubbed. This was 'de poo pussons' table', for it was an old custom that food should be given to all and sundry who might be in need of it. At this table many a vagrant obtained rest and refreshment before continuing on his way. On that verandah, too, stood the dripstones which filtered the drinking water. Large hollowed-out blocks of limestone, they stood, one above the other, within a square enclosure surrounded by a trellis with ferns about the base. The top stone was filled with water from the wells twice a day and the water slowly percolated through into the lower one, through which it again percolated into a big clay cooler that held ten gallons. With a copper dipper on a long handle a number of pitchers – or 'guglets' as they were called – were filled and these were kept on a ledge outside the dining-room. How cool and sweet that water was, for both the wells at Piedmont were fed by an underground spring and the 'guglets' too were porous. The notes the dripstones played were like a fairy melody as the drops tinkled from one to the other, and finally, echoingly, into the cooler underneath.

There was no water supply in San Fernando, and in the dry season, as water was very scarce, the poor would come morning and afternoon to beg a bucketful from the Piedmont wells. The padlocked tops were then opened by the gardener and all would come forward in an orderly line to receive their ration.

Because of the water shortage there were no plunge-baths in the houses around San Fernando, most households making do with hip-baths: but my grandfather had installed what was known as an 'English' bath in a room upstairs, which was considered immensely luxurious. It was encased in mahogany in typical Victorian style, which I thought most imposing; but what really thrilled me was the fact that there was a stained glass window at its foot, so that as I lay in the bath the sun, shining through the coloured panes, cast splashes of mauve and orange, crimson and blue upon the water, and by suitable movement I could acquire purple legs and a golden stomach, and similar combinations and permutations.

There was, however, one thing at Piedmont which cast a shadow over my mother's happiness. Her father's old home, nearby La Coulée, no longer belonged to her family. It had been sold in most unhappy circumstances some years before my birth. That story I must now relate.

CHAPTER EIGHT

Nini and Marie

My mother's great-grandfather, Maurice de Rostang d'Ancézune, was one of seven brothers, the sons of a nobleman with estates near Carpentras in southern France. Ruined by the agrarian disturbances and terrorism that prevailed for years before the Revolution, his parents had abandoned their properties in despair, the family had been scattered, and the brothers were not to see each other again for many years.

In desperation Maurice had turned his eyes to the West Indies as a possible new home, for his family owned large properties in Haiti; but already the revolutionary seed was yielding a bloody harvest there and in the other French islands of Martinique and Guadeloupe; and all the other islands belonged either to England, with whom France was at war, or to Spain, which allowed no foreign settlers – except in Trinidad.

So he and his wife had decided to come to Trinidad. Fortunately Trinidad in many ways was the most propitious place of all, for it was fertile, beautiful and almost completely undeveloped. By 1773, after nearly three hundred years of undisputed Spanish rule, its tiny population consisted of merely 173 adult male Spanish colonists with their families, a few negro slaves, and some hundreds of aboriginal Carib Indians. It was neglected because Spain possessed infinitely richer and more alluring territories in South and Central America, and in Cuba and Puerto Rico, so that for Spaniards Trinidad was merely a staging point for galleons that sailed on to Cartagena and Panama, Mexico, Peru or Havana; or for adventurers seeking the fabled gold-paved city of El Dorado, which was said to lie far up the river Orinoco, whose vast delta pours the mud of the Andes into the Atlantic ocean a mere ten miles or so south of the island.

In 1783 the King of Spain had approved a cedula opening the island to settlement by other nationalities, and immediately this was taken up by Frenchmen of all political persuasions – in such numbers that before long the island had a predominantly French population and a French culture.

At first the new arrivals were mainly republicans, but as the Revolution developed they became predominantly royalists, and even in neutral Trinidad there was mutual hostility. Arriving in 1787, Maurice de Rostang took up lands in the south of the island, near San Fernando, then newly founded, and on a precipitous hillside nearby built himself the original Rostang home of La Coulée. He managed to remain aloof from the quarrels, became a member of the Board of Cabildo, the governing body of the island, and was known as Dr de Rostang, for although not formally trained he had considerable medical knowledge, and he gave his services free to all who came, there being no other doctor on the island. When Napoleon became First Consul and France became more settled, he decided to return there, but so popular had he become that the Cabildo was petitioned to influence him to stay.

When Trinidad was captured by the British in 1797 the royalist French families accepted the new regime enthusiastically, for the guillotining of Louis XVI and Marie Antoinette had caused world-wide horror, and England was regarded as the world's principal bulwark against republicanism. Many anglicised their names, and Maurice de Rostang d'Ancézune became Maurice Rostant.

Three years later he died: but so well had he worked that his eldest son, Leon Toussaint, born in 1794, became at the age of twenty-one owner of the fourteen richest estates in Trinidad, and eventually so powerful as to be called the 'King of Couva'.

Alas, this prosperity did not last for ever, even for the 'King', for in the final analysis my grandfather Robert Guppy was right, and cheap labour ruined the sugar planters themselves: they relied upon it instead of modernising their machinery; their costs escalated; sugar beet entered the field in competition with cane; and the British Government's policy of free trade, which enabled British manufactured goods to capture the world's markets, impoverished the West Indies, Britain's earlier source of great wealth.

By 1862 the 'King' was heavily in debt, for it was costing him more to produce his sugar than he could obtain for it, and his estates had shrunk to six. Four successive years of bad crops and low prices finally forced him to sell the lot and to retire.

Fortunately my mother's father had not been directly affected by this. As the youngest son of the family he had had few expectations, but upon marrying soon after returning from completing his education in France, he had been given La Coulée, where my mother and her brothers and sisters were born, and where in moderate prosperity he had lived ever since, for family influence had obtained him an administrative and magisterial appointment in the district, wherein most of the family estates then lay.

But all this was soon to be changed.

Intermarriage in each generation had cemented the French families in Trinidad into a clan which rallied strongly to the support of any one of its members who might be in trouble. Particularly was this the case if scandal threatened the reputation of one of its women.

That a married woman might have 'affairs' was accepted – so long as these were conducted with discretion. But should 'consequences' ensue, the entire clan would unite to conceal the fact from the eyes of the world. It might be reported that Madame So-and-so had given birth to twins, and eyes would be tightly closed to the fact that one of the babies had every appearance of being older than the other; or another infant might be unobtrusively introduced into a family of young children – one extra in the large families of those days would hardly be noticed; nor would any explanation of its presence be forthcoming – it bore the name of its foster-parents and passed as one of their own children.

Such an occurrence is supposed to have taken place in my mother's family, the child in question being a boy named

Philip. I say is 'supposed' to have taken place, for there is no actual evidence that Philip was really such a changeling, and it is possible that the rumours as to his origin were promulgated later to protect the good name of the family and to clear it of responsibility when his behaviour had at last become public.

From childhood Philip seems to have been at odds with his family, and to have flouted all their wishes deliberately. When he grew up, increasingly he associated with people whom they considered disreputable, even outright scoundrels. For a number of years he mortified them by editing a scurrilous news-sheet. In these days we try to avoid moral judgement, but people then were less cautious.

In spite of all this, my mother's family contrived to be kind and forbearing to Philip in the belief that their affection and trust would eventually lead him back to them and their ways. That is the only possible explanation for my grandfather Leonard Rostant's astonishing and ill-judged decision to grant Philip power of attorney over all his property, while he himself departed to Europe on a prolonged visit: a quixotic act which proved disastrous.

My mother's eldest sister, Anna Fitzsimmons, had died within a few years of her marriage and left no children. Of her two brothers the younger, after an education at Prior Park, had entered the medical profession, married in England and never returned to Trinidad. The elder studied to be a mining engineer, but failed to pass his examinations because he refused to exert himself in pursuit of anything but pleasure, then returned to Trinidad to idle away his time for some years until he eventually betook himself to the Venezuelan gold fields, where he remained until just before his death. After them came another girl, Eugenie; and nearly ten years later, and shortly before their mother's death, there was born the last of the family, my aunt Marie.

Eugenie, or Nini as she was called, had been a lovely child, but at some period during her infancy she sustained an injury to her spine. It was thought that she had fallen from the verandah at La Coulée and that the nurse had concealed the fact. As soon as the injury was discovered she was taken to doctors innumerable, but no treatment had any effect and she remained deformed throughout her life. The tragedy was all the greater because not only did she possess a beautiful face and a spritely wit, but a voice of outstanding quality.

Her father, recognising the quality of her voice and anxious to do all he could to compensate her for her misfortune, decided to resign from his job and take her to Paris where she could best be trained. So with rash but characteristic impetuosity he bestowed a power of attorney on his brother Philip, and left for Europe with Nini and Marie.

There Nini's voice was pronounced good enough for opera, and she was persuaded that with carefully arranged draperies her deformity would not be noticeable on the stage. Then, just as all promised so well, news reached them that Philip had borrowed on the value of the estate, mortgaging it up to the hilt, and had lost everything. At once Leonard Rostant and his two daughters hurried back to Trinidad, where Leonard found that only by the sale of all he possessed could he save himself from bankruptcy.

So La Coulée passed out of the family and Leonard Rostant came to live in Port-of-Spain, where he rented a small bungalow in a street off the Savannah almost immediately behind our house. It was here that I have my first memories of my maternal grandfather and my two aunts.

Nini was in her early twenties and Marie in her 'teens. With inflexible pride Nini concealed her disappointment behind a façade of gaiety, but now there was a sharp and bitter ironic edge to her wit. Youthful Marie adjusted herself good-humouredly to their changed circumstances and seemed unaffected. But their father had neither Marie's youth nor Nini's resolution. His life was in ruins. He who had been a man of property and of scrupulous honour was now deprived of the former; and despite the fact that he had reduced himself to penury to meet his obligations he felt that the latter was besmirched. In the little bungalow close-huddled among others he abandoned himself to grief and bitter self-reproach at the spacious days so rapidly, foolishly, and irretrievably lost.

The news of the catastrophe brought an offer from a relative in France to pay for the completion of Nini's musical education. Nini herself refused it. She was the mainstay of the little household and she felt it her duty to remain with her father and to look after her young sister. So she busied herself contriving to make ends meet, her talent constrained to the narrow channel of trying to cheer up her father by singing the French and Italian songs he loved to hear. Marie would come running home each evening from school, her piquant little face full of eagerness for life, but not even she tripping about the house or chatting cheerfully as she sat sewing to save money on her dresses could rouse their father from his gloom.

Then came yet another cruel blow. Two years later the relative in France died, leaving legacies to both Nini and Marie, and there was general rejoicing at this change in fortune. But in the midst of it a letter arrived from the doctor brother in England to say that he had been living beyond his means and that his creditors were threatening to foreclose. He had a wife and two children, one of whom was Nini's godchild and the other Marie's. Neither hesitated for an instant: each made her legacy over to him, and before long he was on his feet again. But at the time this final humiliation was too much for their father, who was immensely proud of his doctor son, and it broke his heart.

At his death his pension ceased and my aunts were left virtually without means of support. Their uncle, Maurice Rostant, offered them a home, but he was already supporting several other elderly relations and the prospect of such an existence offended Nini's independent spirit. She announced her determination to work for her living and that of Marie.

The family was aghast – the whole clan was shaken to its remotest ramifications: she, Eugenie, the daughter of Leonard Rostant, working for her living! What an indignity! And anyhow, at what would she work? If she must solace herself with some occupation, then let her live at her Uncle Maurice's and take young pupils for music lessons and singing. To this Nini answered with finality that never would she so prostitute her talent, that she disliked children anyway, and that she and Marie would exist on no-one's bounty.

None the less the outlook was unpromising. Apart from teaching there was in those days little opportunity for a white woman to earn a living in Trinidad. But eventually she

obtained a job of post-mistress and registrar of births and
deaths for the district of New Town, Port-of-Spain. It was
poorly paid and undistinguished work, but at least it offered
independence. They moved into an even smaller bungalow,
to which they gave an air of elegance with the few old pieces
of furniture they had saved. And 'Zabette and one of her
daughters, called Mrs Clark, who had been in my father's
household since she was born, took it upon themselves to
look after them, often without pay.

Nini made a great jest of being employed to sell stamps, but
she sat behind the little counter and conducted the business
with aplomb, and was far too proud to let anyone suspect the
depth of her humiliation or the toll that her frustrations and
disappointments were taking of her. But her wit grew barbed
with a polished malice, and as the years went by ridicule
increasingly became her sword and shield.

Each of these catastrophes naturally had its repercussions in
our household. My mother's emotional nature responded
readily enough to everyone's troubles, but when the victims
were of her own family, her reactions were all the more
intense. The series of misfortunes which befell her father and
sisters, and her father's death, filled her with grief such as she
had never known before, made worse by the fact that at each
disaster every member of the clan would call in turn to lament
– or to gloat, as Nini said. No sooner had she begun to recover
a little from the visit of one old cousin of remote degree than
that of another would plunge her into despondency again.
Her quick smile faded altogether from her lips, her eyes were
often red with weeping, and no more was her small, true
voice heard singing *Sweet Alice Benbolt*, *Au Clair de Lune* or
other of the songs she loved.

Something had to be done, and at last my father decided to
take her to Europe. They had long promised themselves a trip
on the Continent. They had had several invitations to stay
with scientist colleagues in France, Germany and Switzerland
of which he was eager to avail himself, while my mother, who
had not been to Paris for years, was longing to see it again. It
was already midsummer, so they must wait until spring:
nevertheless the prospect of travelling in countries new to

her, and of meeting interesting people everywhere, had an immediate tonic effect upon her, and not only did she begin to make plans for the trip, but she cast round in her mind as to how it could be made to benefit those left behind.

Soon she had everything arranged: while she and my father were away, her sisters would live in our house and take charge of us children. It would be a wonderful respite for them from that horrid little bungalow.

And so it was that at a very early age I came to receive my first lessons in cruelty and humiliation.

CHAPTER NINE

At the Misses Cadis

To my chagrin I missed much of the preparation for my parents' departure for Europe, for with the advent of my sixth birthday it was decided that my education should begin and the first step was taken in that haphazard and spasmodic process.

Each morning at half-past eight Estelle conducted me to the bungalow of the Misses Cadis in Marli Street, and I and the other dozen or so of their pupils, hung up our hats on the verandah while our nurses departed in a chattering group to return for us at eleven-thirty.

The Misses Cadis could hardly have been out of their thirties when I made my appearance at their kindergarten, and already they were firmly established in spinsterhood. They had been good-looking in their girlhood and they had had every opportunity of making suitable marriages, but 'they had played their cards badly,' so it was said, and mothers of marriageable daughters used to point to them as sad examples of girls who did that. They had considered themselves highly superior, and as a result admirers had dropped away one by one. The death of their parents had left them with very slender means. It became essential to supplement them, which they did in as genteel a manner as possible.

They were still good-looking, pale, with clear-cut features, but their appearance was not improved by the way in which they scraped their hair into tight buns or by the severity of the clothes they wore. The elder walked with a very erect carriage, her elbows pressed close to her sides, her thin hands clasped together. The younger, who had suffered an accident some years before, was a semi-cripple and spent most of her time in a wheelchair.

Their pupils were divided into two classes. The younger, myself among them, were taught by the crippled sister. Her wheelchair was drawn up at one side of a table in the centre of the sitting-room, and we children sat on stools around its other three sides. We recited the alphabet and formed its letters laboriously on our slates with squeaky slate pencils; together we counted up to one hundred or chanted such sentences as 'The Dog sat on the Mat' and 'The Cat ate the Rat'. We also threaded beads on bits of string, and worked useless little mats in cross-stitch with Berlin wool. Halfway through the morning we were refreshed with a glass of lemonade and a biscuit.

I doubt if I had been conscious that such a thing as an alphabet existed before I joined the kindergarten. Having taught myself to read without being aware of it, the dreary task of learning how I did it, and of being degraded to spelling out sentences of five words none of which contained more than three letters, I found a considerable indignity. That I could spell none of the words I read so glibly troubled me not at all. I had liked the idea of going to school, but I soon grew weary of the morning's routine and for the first time in my short life discovered the meaning of boredom.

The eight children sitting around the table were of my own age, yet all were far less mentally developed than I – 'more babyish', I thought. My mind and fingers were nimbler than theirs, so that I had completed any task before they were fairly launched upon it, and while they laboured on I was left with nothing to do. I had scanned each picture on the wall until I knew every detail of it by heart; I knew the smallest blemish on each article of furniture in the room; I was familiar with every mannerism of Miss Cadis and every expression on her face.

Swinging my heels, mourning my lost freedom, my thoughts flew back to our house and to all that was occurring there. The shade under the saman would be deep at this hour . . . Marie might be coming in, eager and vital . . . She and my mother would be engrossed in examining fashion papers, discussing materials . . . My father would be making a new cabinet and the shavings would be curling crisply from his plane . . . And here was I sitting on a hard stool, doing nothing, inert and numb.

Then I made a discovery. Along the edge of the verandah stood a row of plants in pots. These were watered before we arrived so that there were always a number of drops still spangling the leaves. Gazing at them one day, admiring their iridescence in the sunshine, I found that if I stared at a single drop with sufficient intentness it seemed to grow and swell, while upon myself there descended a delicious drowsiness, in which condition I could sail away to far horizons in a sort of waking dream. Morning after morning I sought refuge in this Nirvana. At first Miss Cadis had to rap smartly on the table to command my attention, but soon I succeeded in keeping sufficient contact with reality to enable one part of my mind to respond to her unexacting demands, while all the rest was free to voyage on the enchanted ocean of my imagination.

At the end of my first term Miss Cadis reported that although I was inclined to be inattentive she felt sure I would show more interest in my lessons later on. At the end of my second term her report expressed much the same sentiments, and my mother took me to task. I defended myself by explaining that I was *miserable* in the class with the small children, and if I could be moved into the higher class it would make all the difference.

In the higher class they were learning the multiplication table, which intrigued me, unmathematical though I was, and am; they were reading about King Alfred and the cakes, Canute and the sea, Bruce and the spider: stories with which I was already familiar, but which, nevertheless, still held an interest. They were learning, too, that London was on the Thames and that part of England was called the 'Black Country' which awoke my curiosity. I had been in London and seen the Thames, which was more than any of the other children in the kindergarten had done, and here was I kept to the First Primer with its ridiculous little tales and silly verses like the one which began:

Dear child with soul as white
As the page on which you write . . .

My mother sent a note to Miss Cadis asking if I could not be put in the advanced class, but in reply she said that, while she agreed I ought to be, it was reserved for children over seven and that to put me in it over the heads of my classmates would offend their mothers and was therefore out of the question. My father gave a great laugh when he read this.

'An attitude toward education which I hope is unique', he remarked.

I cautiously suggested that I might give up going to Miss Cadis.

'Oh no!' said my mother. 'However little you may learn there, it's good for you to be with other children. You're too fond of mooning about by yourself.'

Ever since I could remember, Estelle had taken me out in the afternoon to meet other children of my own age. We toddlers had been disregarded by the older children, whose nurses allowed them the freedom of flying kites or playing round games in the Savannah. Now my mother considered that I was old enough to join in such games, and my reluctance to do so mystified and irritated her. That I was prone to the lonely child's diffidence in the company of other children she could understand, but that there might be essential differences between me and them was beyond her comprehension. If anyone had hazarded such a suggestion she would instantly have replied: 'Then the sooner she alters the better for herself and every one else!' It was customary for children to have playmates, and any deviation from the normal, especially in a girl, must be discouraged. It was not that I disliked playing rounders or 'Oranges and Lemons' in the Savannah: on the contrary I enjoyed it. The trouble was that once the games were over I found I had little in common with my playfellows, and could only stand about feeling awkward, shy and out of place among them.

'Spending the day' at one another's houses was also a pastime in which parents encouraged their children. With few exceptions I was not partial to these outings: the youthful hostess did not seek to entertain her guest, but the guest was expected to subordinate herself to the whims of her hostess; the house and its inmates were strange to me, and away from my own environment I felt defenceless and vulnerable. That I returned exhausted from such visits my mother soon recognised, and it was therefore only when invitations came from particular friends of ours that she insisted upon accepting them.

'I simply can't refuse,' she would say as I proclaimed my unwillingness to go. 'Besides it's a compliment that you should be asked – Mrs So-and-so is exceedingly particular whom she allows her children to mix with. There isn't another child in the place who wouldn't be delighted to go.'

I had no words to explain my reluctance to do what other children delighted in, nor would my mother have understood that though many – perhaps most – children enjoyed the constant companionship of their fellows, others, like myself, grew quickly exhausted, and only frequent spells alone in the realms of their own imaginations could renew their nervous vitality. Still less would my mother have sympathised with the things that *really* absorbed me, and which often continued from day to day so that I hated losing the thread – like watching a bird build her nest or feed her young, seeing the big iguana that lived in the saman tree emerge to lie along one of the branches, or trying to find the nest of the leaf-cutting ants that were pillaging our roses. Things like these, trivial to others, were to me so absorbing that the thought of missing them filled me with a sense of irretrievable loss.

CHAPTER TEN

Nini takes Charge

━━━━━◦◦◦◦━━━━━

Upon the departure of my parents to England my aunts came to stay at our house and take charge, and its whole atmosphere underwent a complete change. Meals were seldom punctual; relations and friends were in and out all day long, and French, not English, was generally spoken.

Marie was now aged twenty-four and Nini thirty-one. As Lent was over, the usual round of parties was beginning again, so that when my aunts were not out of an evening a succession of young men and women came in. They danced or gathered around the piano singing *The Tin Gee-Gee*, *Daddy wouldn't buy me a Bow-wow-wow*, *Killaloo* and the other popular songs of the day. It was gay and friendly. Had things been just a little different I should have delighted in such liveliness. Had I been less jealously inclined I should not have been so resentful of the changes that were made. But I was piqued because the drawing-room furniture was rearranged, my father's chair and reading-lamp banished, and the table on which the lamp had stood pushed into a corner. I was resentful because my mother's precious Dresden tea-set which she prized so highly was being constantly used and getting chipped and broken. I was jealous because these and other changes of a like nature made me feel a stranger in my own home, in which I was now relegated to a position of complete insignificance.

But even these things, galling though they were to the profound conservatism of a sensitive child, would not have assumed the proportions they did had not matters gone awry between Nini and myself, as a result of which I became all too often the butt of her peculiarly French powers of ridicule – that pungent ridicule to which, indeed, the French owe so much of their reputation for wit. She used this weapon only upon me, and against it I was too small to have any defences. Nor could my brothers or sisters do much to help me, for she was too clever.

There were occasions when she could be very charming, but I grew to mistrust them, for I learned how swiftly and unexpectedly they could end in some jibe at my expense, with the result that I was never at ease with her, but always suspicious and on my guard, which, of course, only served to irritate and provoke her.

I had no conception then of the problems, inhibitions, and frustrations which had embittered Nini, nor could I be expected to know that those who find themselves differentiated from the rest of mankind by a physical deformity, if they do not actually hate their fellows, are often sourly disposed towards them, and often derive a warped satisfaction from inflicting pain. So it was with Nini – and I provided a handy victim. When visitors were present she would hail my entry into the room with:

'Ah! Here is our Bébé, her father's "Little Lass".' Then with a ripple of laughter: 'No, do not mistake me: I said "Little Lass", – *not* "Little Ass!" '

Which never failed to raise a laugh. Then: 'Such a pity she has such rat's-tails! If only one could graft some of Imp's lovely curls on to this little head! *La pauvre petite-là*! Ah well, perhaps *le bon Dieu* will bless her in some way or other which He has not revealed as yet!'

Marie would try to soothe my hurts as well as she could, putting an arm about me affectionately and whispering:

'Never mind, *chérie* – Nini is only joking. She wanted you to laugh! See? So don't be unhappy.' But I knew better.

The contrast between the two sisters was never more striking than when they performed at the musical evenings they loved to give. At most times Nini's eyes, shaded by their heavy lashes, glinted with a suspicious watchfulness, with disdain, arrogance or derision; but when she sang all these gave place to a tenderness that melted one's very bones and made one conscious only of her beauty: one was oblivious of all else, nothing mattered but the miracle of melody that was her voice. So exquisitely, so effortlessly did it pour forth. And under its influence she herself stood transformed. She held her elegant head high. The contours of her face were soft and perfect.

To Marie playing the piano was a means of expressing merely the essential joyousness of her nature. Sitting before it, her upright little body was vibrant with the music which her broad hands, with their short, blunt fingers, produced as they flew over the keyboard. She played with a dashing, light-hearted abandon, often improvising recklessly, tossing a roguish quip over her shoulder or flashing a sudden glance. If in her eagerness she struck a wrong note, with a little squeal she would cry 'zut!' and obliterate it in a resounding chord.

It was Marie's influence that prevented all our servants leaving, for no-one is more conservative than a domestic servant of whatever race or colour, and they resented the changes in our household as much as I did myself. Nor could they endure Nini's sarcastic tongue. And they hated Mrs Clark, who had come with her and had at once adopted airs of superiority. Instead of the smiles and good-nature which had formerly prevailed, there were now glum looks and dark mutterings, and one morning I found Augustus Bellborder on his knees beside a burn made by a cigarette-end on his precious drawing-room floor. He was on the verge of tears – too deeply stricken even for one of his paroxysms of temper – and in the weeks that followed that blemish became as much of an obsession with him as did the bloodstain with Lady Macbeth. These feelings he communicated to me so thoroughly that I could never enter the room without my eyes fastening on that blackened scorch with an upsurging of anger and grief hardly less intense than Augustus Bellborder's own.

I missed my mother sorely, but I pined unceasingly for my father. The workshop was a void, empty of his song, of the crisp swishing of his plane, the rasping of his saw and the tapping of his hammer. There were no games of an evening, no Combies to earn. But, worst of all, his study had been locked by Nini and she kept the key.

We had our first real brush over his books, to which she refused to give me access.

'But he *always* let me have any I wanted,' I protested vehemently. 'And you know it perfectly well!'

'That was your father's affair – I can't accept the responsibility. If he had wished you to have the books he would have said so.'

'He would have done if he had thought you wouldn't let me have them.'

'Well it's a good thing you can't. They are not the sort of books for a child to read.'

This was too much and I flamed out passionately:

'If my father thought they were, then they *were*! And he's much more clever than you!'

'How dare you speak to me like that! You want a good thrashing!'

Without his books and without my father himself I felt like a lost soul. Life seemed aimless, drained of colour, and the days, always so swift in flight before, now seemed unending. Tears were continually smarting behind my eyes and I was never rid of the dull ache of desolation in my heart. When I heard Samuel chopping the kindling of a morning and the black coffee going to my aunts' rooms instead of to my parents', I would sob into my pillow. No coffee-sugar, no scrambling into my parents' bed to lie cosily and listen to the familiar sounds that heralded the opening of a new day.

In my distress I withdrew more and more into myself and began to experience a strange spiritual isolation. The roots of the saman tree were now my only sanctuary. A sense of unreality descended upon me. I came to feel a peculiar detachment from my surroundings as though I were a visitant from another sphere. Into my mind seeped the questions: 'Why are you here?' 'Where do you belong?' I would tread the ground feeling as though I were walking on cotton-wool, and when I looked down the earth seemed a long way off, as if I had grown to a great height and become attenuated and insubstantial as a wraith. I was frequently beset by the conviction that I had lived through some incident that was occurring before, and waited with a strained expectancy for the next scene to unfold. I make no attempt to explain any of these sensations. I write of them simply because they happened, and in the same spirit I relate a strange experience that befell me.

I had always been fascinated by flight. Watching the movements of birds engrossed me, whether it was the soaring flight of swifts, the joyous sundown exercises of pigeons or the effortless vigil of the vultures, minute specks stationary against the sky. As I contemplated birds in flight I was able to induce the same trance-like state, as when I had contemplated the sparkling drop of water at Miss Cadis', and with my mind similarly detached I accomplished fantastic journeys in their company. From there it was but a short step to the conviction that, if I concentrated sufficiently upon it, I also should be able to fly – in fact as well as in imagination. I was convinced that it was only a matter of knowing the correct method of breathing, of urging the body upwards with the will, and of performing certain movements with the arms, all in coordination. Quite suddenly it was born in upon me what I must do to succeed: I must have a straight pitch along which to run with no obstacles to impede me, and I must go from north to south – why this last I cannot tell, I simply knew it must be so.

The long cement way which ran from the bathroom, past the kitchen and servants' rooms, to the stables and coach house was ideal. It went from north to south, and to one of my diminutive size it seemed a very long stretch indeed. I chose early evening as the time for practice. Under normal circumstances that was the time when I should be out with Estelle in the Savannah, but no-one noticed now whether I went out of an afternoon or not, and Estelle was only too pleased to escape her duty and gossip idly in the yard instead. At that hour, too, my aunts were occupied with their social engagements, and Mrs Clark indoors.

Starting from the bathroom door there first came an interlude to attune the mind; then I would begin to run – north to south – on my toes, light and swift, drawing my breath deep into my lungs and making appropriate movements of arms and shoulders . . . Then back to the starting point at slow pace, mind intent . . . Again and again swift, light, run . . . lift! . . . *lift!*

Occasionally one of the servants would glance my way and ask idly of another:

'What do dis chil'? What be dis new game she playin'?'

Waking or sleeping the determination to fly became fixed in my mind. At night I soared into sleep, and sleeping soared on, and when I awoke I knew with detailed accuracy what the trees and houses looked like from above. Birds did not accompany me on these dream-flights. I was quite alone, and the sense of freedom, of space and peace, was exquisite.

One evening Estelle was sitting on her little bench under the frangipani tree working desultorily at a piece of crochet, with Lavinia and a friend beside her. The air was soft and tranquil, and the perfume of the frangipani flowers lay heavily upon it. It was near to sunset – that brief tropical interlude of fading light and brightening colours when all nature seems to pause and wait, in awe of the approaching night. I seemed to absorb that tenseness and expectancy as I stood at my starting point; a feeling of exultation filled me and I knew with a sudden convincing clarity that I was on the threshold of achieving my dream.

I rejoiced in the chill of the cement under my bare feet as I stood with my heels lifted and toes pressing down, my elbows close against my sides, my forearms turned outwards, my hands opened horizontally. I was waiting for a signal which I knew would come to me . . . to launch myself forward.

It came, on a sweet current of air: my toes touched the ground a dozen times or so, my hands rose and fell, with my indrawn breath came a sense of buoyancy, and like a feather wafted upward I was off the ground . . . sailing through space . . . When I touched down again it was with a small jolt and quick, jerky steps, as when one alights from a moving vehicle.

My experience could not have endured more than an instant, in distance a few paces, but while it lasted I dwelt in infinity. The sensation was indescribable, rapturous, mysterious, frightening. As I write it is with me still.

I was still in the grip of my emotions when, as from a distance, I heard cries of fear. With a rush of feet and swirl of skirts Estelle's arms were clutching me. Her eyes were wide and her voice hollow as she cried:

'What is dis t'ing yo' done, chil'? Dis is a bad t'ing yo' do! Yo' is *nebber, nebber* to do dis t'ing again! – yo' hearin' what I say?'

I could feel her heart thudding as she clasped me. Though still bemused and dazed, the urgency of her fear communicated itself to me: with a twist of my body I escaped and sped across the yard, past the gaping Lavinia and her friend, round the house to my tree. Behind its tall roots I sank down, my heart racing painfully.

But I never flew again either in fact or fancy. I had touched something which filled me with ecstacy – yet filled me also with a sense of dread.

CHAPTER ELEVEN

The Surprise Packet

At last September came and I could say to myself: 'Next month they will be here!'

I was making a 'surprise packet' with which to greet my father. I had saved up my pocket money and bought a box of pink note-paper and stitched the sheets into a book. With Marie's aid in spelling I had written out a story of my own invention and illustrated it with coloured transfers and pencil drawings. Then I had got a letter from him in which my father said: 'We are taking the first mail-boat in October and will be with you on the twenty-first of that month. Your mother has bought you a doll, which is called Adelina after Madame Patti. She says 'Mama' and 'Papa', she can be dressed and undressed, and there is a trunk suitable to her size, with a whole outfit for her in it including mittens and a parasol. I have a present for you, too. But what will be nicer than anything will be to see you again . . .'

The morning dawned when I could tell myself 'They have sailed!' I could snuggle down in bed and listen to Samuel chopping the kindling and tell myself that only fourteen times more would he do that before I could spring out of bed and race to their room for coffee-sugar.

My aunts had begun to collect their possessions from the various parts of the house. The furniture was replaced in its original position. Each day when I returned from Miss Cadis' I would shoot glances around me and note the heartening signs of a return to normal. A mule-cart came to fetch away my aunts' heavy luggage, and then the work of scrubbing, cleaning and polishing began. The servants set to work jubilantly.

'Dis day nex' week, please Gawd, all we own folks will be done come,' they told each other, and anyone else who entered the yard.

Only Augustus Bellborder was as lugubrious as ever as he drooped and muttered over the charred spot on the drawing-room floor. He scowled at it with frightful grimaces, as though hoping to frighten it away. Then one day an idea flashed into his mind. With a sound like the whinnying of a horse he suddenly dropped the polishing broom and pounded out into the yard at a shambling run, leaving Samuel gaping with astonishment.

'Which place he done gorn?' he questioned vaguely, and since no answer was forthcoming, propped himself against the wall and philosophically awaited developments.

Presently Augustus returned with Laycock. They knelt beside the scorch and held a whispered consultation. At last Laycock stood up, nodded his head emphatically and announced:

'He gwine come out. I'se gwine get he out good-good.'

With the utmost reluctance I started for school. When it was over I ran the whole way home and straight into the drawing-room. The burn was gone! A little patch slightly lighter in tone than the rest of the floor was all that remained to show where once it had been. My heart welled up with relief. And next day, after further attentions from Augustus, even that little patch had disappeared, and for the first time for weeks a smile reappeared on Augustus' features.

I had asked to be allowed to go with my aunts to the quay to meet my parents, but though Marie backed my request and Ruth said she would look after me, Nini refused to hear of it.

'The child will only be a nuisance,' she said irritably. 'There will be a lot of people there, and on these occasions children are only in the way.'

I was speechless with indignation and resentment, and departed to the saman to think the matter out. I was determined to go in spite of Nini; the problem was – how? The tram-car would take me nearly to the wharf, but a ticket cost threepence and I had no money at all, nor hope of getting any by tomorrow morning. I should have to walk. But it was a long way – nearly two miles – and quite apart from the fact that white children did not go about unattended, the way led through what was known as a 'disorderly quarter', the very idea of which filled me with misgivings though I was determined not to let it deter me.

By discreet inquiries I learned that it would take about half an hour to reach the Customs House and that the launch from the mail-boat would be alongside soon after half-past eight. To make sure of getting out of the house undetected I decided to leave it soon after daylight and wait in the Savannah until I heard the prison clock strike eight.

As Estelle undressed me that night I asked her what clothes I was to wear on the morrow and where they were.

'Yo' bes' white sailor-suit, darlin'.'

'And where is it?'

'Lawd ha' mercy, chil' what-fo' yo' wantin' to know dat?'

'Tell me, Estelle, please, please! I want to know. Are my shoes and socks and everything all ready?'

'Yo' is too glad yo' payrents is comin', eh darlin'? I is well glad meself.'

'But my clothes for tomorrow, Estelle?'

'*Chutt*, chil'! How yo' does set yo' min' 'pon a t'ing! Yo' does weary-down a pusson! I is gwine put eb'ryt'ing dis night fo' de bottom shelf o' de wardrobe in yo' room.'

I released a long breath of satisfaction. Then another thought occurred to me: I must have something to eat before I left in the morning.

'Estelle, I'm hungry.'

'*Eh bien!* I did tell yo' yo' gwine be hungry befo' night when yo' no mo' dan pick at yo' food dis eb'nin'. What yo' is wantin' to eat? . . . Get in yo' bed den, an' I gwine bring yo' bread and butter wid brown sugar. Yo' wish fo' dat, honey?'

'And a banana too,' I suggested.

When with the first hint of dawn I awoke after a restless and agitated night I ate my hoard thankfully. In the half darkness I dressed myself, making an indifferent job of tying the sailor knot of my tie. I tiptoed out of the house, slipped through the gate and ran as fast as I could into the Savannah where I seated myself on the roots of a silk-cotton tree and awaited the striking of the prison clock. As I sat there expectantly my courage began to ebb, so that the moment the clock struck I jumped up quickly and started on my way as resolutely and at as fast a pace as possible. But I felt very lonely and apprehensive when I had to turn my back on the Savannah's friendly green expanse and take the street which led into the town, and to bolster up my morale I had to keep reminding myself how triumphantly I was scoring off Nini.

At first the long street before me was bordered with pleasant houses set in bright gardens, but with disconcerting abruptness its whole character changed. Dilapidated shanties erupted at all angles to the pavement's edge, the closed shutters of which were now being thrown open while through the sagging doors the occupants could be glimpsed yawning and stretching after their night's sleep. The thunder of wheels, the clatter of galloping hooves, a cracking whip, and a mule-cart dashed past, the driver standing with straddled legs and shouting at the animal as he flogged it. A pack of curs appeared from nowhere to pursue the cart with frantic barking, while half-clad men and women craned out of windows to see what was the cause of this disturbance. Suddenly one of them cried out:

'Eh-eh! look at dat white chil'!' then shouted to a man on the other side of the road: 'Stop she! Ask she which part she gwine.'

To my horror a huge negro stepped in front of me, grinning, and barred my way.

'Let me pass,' I said, trying to assume the imperious air which Nini could command so easily. The negro grinned still more widely.

'Which part yo' is gwine? Whose chil' yo' be? Tell me dat.'

'Let me pass,' I repeated, quaveringly. Perhaps he meant to be kind, but I was now getting frightened.

He gave a loud guffaw, echoed from all sides from the crowd that was collecting now, hemming me in, from the ragged children prancing around me. They gaped and jabbered, and the smell of their unwashed skin and clothes was rank and nauseating. My knees went weak, my stomach seemed to cleave to my spine. With all my heart I longed for

Yseult aged 11
from a drawing by Theodora Walter

Robert Guppy, aged 84, in
the Legislative Council, 1892

Amelia Guppy on her return
from the Orinoco Expedition
in 1872

Alice (*left*) with Prince George, later King George V (*right*).
In the centre Sir Napier Broome, Governor of Trinidad, and Lady Broome, 1892

A group of 'Tantans' going for a walk in
the country near Uncle Maurice's house

Maurice Rostant
*from a sketch
by Gerard Rostant*

Aunt Nini Rostant

Estelle to appear. The big negro man took a step towards me
with his hand outstretched, intending to grip me by the arm. I
felt my face grow stiff as though it was moulded in cement,
while everything began to spin about me. I think I must have
been on the point of fainting when there came the brisk clatter
of a trotting horse, the padded rumble of rubber-tired wheels,
and a clear voice called out:

'Hi! What's all this?'

I did not – I could not – turn round, or even move, and there
followed a small hiatus in my memory. The next thing I
remember is the newcomer, an Englishman, taking my hand
in his and saying:

'Come along now, everything is all right.'

Relief ran over my body in soft waves and the next moment
he lifted me into a high dog-cart, got in beside me and
gathered up the reins. He drove a little distance in silence,
then asked in a tone of mild inquiry, as though the whole
episode had been the most natural thing in the world:

'Where would you like me to take you?'

No word of reproof! No questions! My relief and gratitude
gave me back some self-confidence, and I was able to still a
quivering lip and reply:

'To the Customs House, please.'

'Going to meet the mail-boat? he inquired gravely.

I began primly, to still the quaver in my voice: 'Yes; my
parents are arriving from England . . .' Then I trailed into
silence.

'I see. And the rest of the family has gone on ahead?' he
suggested, helping me out tactfully. I nodded gratefully.
'Well' – he drew out his watch – 'it's a quarter past eight, so we
have plenty of time. When we get there, would you like me to
stay with you until the launch comes alongside, or leave you
to join the others?'

'Leave me to join the others, please.'

'Well, you know best,' he murmured smiling, 'but won't
there be a bit of bother about this . . . er . . . adventure of
yours?'

But I knew now that Nini's reign was over. I felt suddenly,
joyously, free. I looked up into his face and laughed happily.

'Aunt Nini *will* be cross when she sees me, but she won't be able to say anything because lots of other people will be there. And besides, you see, she won't be in charge of me any longer.'

'Of course,' he said, and his eyes twinkled.

Then I gave a cry of annoyance.

'I've been so *stupid*!' I said. 'I made a surprise packet for my father – I meant to bring it to give him, but I've forgotten it.'

At that he laughed aloud.

'A surprise packet! You'll be that yourself, I fancy!'

In front of the Customs House he pulled up, got out of the trap and, coming round to my side, swung me down in his arms.

'We'll go in together, shall we? And as soon as we see your party I'll leave you. Is that correct?'

We entered the Customs House hand in hand. There were several groups of people, talking and laughing, and some carrying bouquets. I felt very excited.

'Look! There are my aunts over there,' I cried, and, forgetting my manners, pointed.

We shook hands gravely, and he gave mine a friendly squeeze; then, as he turned to walk away he raised his hat to me exactly as though I had been grown up. That made me feel so tremendously elated that without a moment's hesitation I ran over to our little group and gave Marie's skirt a tug to announce my presence.

'*Mon dieu*, child!' she exclaimed. 'But how did you get here? *Tu es l'enfant terrible!*'

'I'm a surprise packet!' I declared, dancing with delight.

At that moment a voice cried that the launch was alongside, and Nini had only time to cast me a withering glance before everyone surged forward.

Whether it was the French influence or the island's own exotic atmosphere, or simply because, being a small community, people were drawn intimately together, or whether it was a mingling of all three, in Trinidad every happy event was transformed into a festival.

So it was with my parents' return: the house was filled with baskets and bowls of roses and orchids and lilies, each with its card of welcome or invitation. Luncheon, normally just a family affair, was today a banquet of my parents' favourite dishes. Everyone talked at the same time, everyone laughed together. The servants scurried about, got in each other's way, giggled – and went unrebuked. The pensioners and protégés had gathered in full force. From the back verandah all could see into the dining-room, and a continuous stream of comments in sibilant whispers which no-one made any attempt to control could be heard issuing from there:

'De Master lookin' grand! He face so fresh and pink. Fo' true he be English!' . . . 'Look – yo' see Madam have a new fashion wid she hair?' . . . Fo' true! An' it takin' she looks well.' . . . 'Watch she laughin'! She be too happy! . . . E-e-e-e! Praise be to Gawd dey done return safe!'

That afternoon carriage after carriage turned into our drive, and my father as well as my mother received the visitors. There were ardent exchanges of compliments, kisses, prolonged handclasps.

When numbers had been somewhat reduced my father made an escape to his study. But my mother was in her element. Surrounded by a circle of her particular friends she talked animatedly of her trip. She had seen the 'Divine Sarah' as Marguerite in *La Dame aux Camélias* – 'My dear! She fell *dead* from the arms of Armand Duval with the lightness of a wisp of chiffon! Exquisite! . . . Patti! What a *superb* voice! . . . the Opera House . . . packed . . . The dresses! . . . I have never seen the women of Paris looking smarter!'

My new red and white sailor suit with kilted skirt – '*Le Dernier Cri* in Berlin', my mother said – was much admired; Adelina was passed from hand to hand and her beauty acclaimed. I fell asleep that evening on my father's knee, with her in my arms. Vaguely I recall his carrying me to bed and tucking in my mosquito-net, as I lay swooning into sleep beside my wonderful new books *Le Morte d'Arthur*, *Treasure Island*, a volume of fairy tales with coloured plates, a birthday book with quotations from Shakespeare . . .

CHAPTER TWELVE
Unexpected Dangers

With my parents' return from England I bade good-bye to the Misses Cadis and the bungalow in Marli Street. It had been arranged that I should share lessons with the two children of one of the Puisne Judges and on six mornings of the week Estelle shepherded me to their house where Miss Annie Bishop, the daughter of the Principal of the Queen's Royal College, taught us.

Annie Bishop's ideas of education were considerably more advanced than those of the Cadis sisters; and she was, besides, a young and cheerful person who possessed the art of gaining and holding a child's attention, and stimulating its interest, so that under her tuition I began to take a real pleasure in my work.

I also found my two companions and the atmosphere of their home congenial. Their father had recently been transferred from some other colony, the climate of which had prevented him from having his wife and children with him, and the children had never been to the tropics before. They were thus devoid of that precocious 'knowingness' which characterised so many children born in the West Indies, and which used to cause me much embarrassment. They, like me, were fond of reading and we had other tastes in common.

Their mother, Mrs Lewis, was a talented woman who wrote books of verse for children which she illustrated herself.

I posed for her on several occasions, but it was Ruth who was her favourite model and who sat for the illustrations of one entire book.

I was very happy both in my work and play, and, when the morning's lessons were over I would frequently spend the remainder of the day at the Lewises, or their two children would spend the afternoon with me. But after some eighteen months Judge Lewis was promoted to another colony and the whole family left Trinidad. Bereft of their friendship I felt very forlorn, and though the children and I kept up a correspondence for some time, we eventually lost touch and I have never seen them since.

It was now decided that I should attend the same school as Ruth – the only private school in Trinidad – which was kept by a lady with the Dickensian name of Bunkle.

The prospect of going to a real school, and of walking to and from it with Ruth and her classmates instead of being led by the hand by Estelle, did something to console me for the loss of the Lewises, as did the new school equipment with which I was provided. I became the proud possessor of a 'two-storied' pencil-box, with a socket to take an india-rubber, and a splendid array of pencils and pens. There was a complete set of school books to write my name in and cover neatly with brown paper; and a new set of holland pinafores were being made for me, each piped with a different colour; and there was a new sailor hat with a dark blue ribbon and the proud name HMS *Triumph*. I was to wear a sun-veil of green gauze, such as all school-girls wore, to protect my eyes and complexion from the sun – a somewhat ludicrous precaution, considering that I ran about bareheaded on all other occasions. And besides all this I was to be allowed a penny a day with which to buy sweetmeats from Matilda, the vendor, during the morning recess.

Sitting beside the seamstress as she made my pinafores I chatted ceaselessly about the wonders of school, but as the day drew nearer I began to suffer qualms of apprehension.

A warmly affectionate child with a generous capacity for admiration, there had been growing in me, before I met the Lewises, a wistful longing for a friend who would be all in all to me and to whom I should be all in all. My friendship with the Lewises had satisfied this longing and at the same time stimulated it. Urgently I hoped now to win the liking of the girls I should be meeting daily. My whole instinct was to please, but my chronic diffidence and self-depreciation created a peculiar form of awkwardness which crippled my every effort to do so, particularly when I was in the company of several children at once. A fear of being unwanted among them prevented me from being my natural self.

My mother had noticed this, and warned me against what she uncomprehendingly called my 'fastidiousness'. Unless I overcame it, she declared, I should be unpopular, and create a lot of unnecessary suffering for myself. I took her admonitions to heart, but they only succeeded in making me more aware of my failings and thereby increasing their intensity. Nor did I derive any help from the girls at Miss Bunkle's. More intensely than most children I needed support. To know that I was liked helped me to have self-assurance. I envied some of the girls at the school their popularity, yet I felt instinctively that it was only superificial and transitory. For the most part they were strident and noisy, and prone to sudden ardent friendships which dissolved equally suddenly into violent quarrels. Such swift transitions from devotion to spite, from tenderness to acrimony, made me withdraw, bewildered, and afraid of becoming the object of the first lest I be made a victim of the second. But that did not prevent me from regretting my shyness and the differences between me and them.

Another cause of division between my companions and myself was my love of reading. Once, having been lent a book I had long wished to read and which the owner wanted back as soon as possible, I took it to school and excusing myself from games, settled down to read it during recess. As a result I was cold-shouldered for weeks afterwards and never really forgiven. Ever afterwards whenever I was asked to join in a game, some girl was sure to cry out:

'Don't ask *her* to play! All she cares about is reading stupid old books!'

While Ruth was at Miss Bunkle's I basked to some extent in the reflected warmth of her popularity, and this made my first six months considerably less unhappy than they would otherwise have been. Ruth was the youngest girl in the senior class, and her quick intelligence kept her at its head. She would sit at her desk with a face flushed by the heat and the intensity of her concentration, her hair spraying about her head in a burnished mass, her tawny eyes wide. Without the slightest exertion on her part she attracted everyone to her. Wherever she moved during the recess girls of all ages hovered around her. Even Miss Bunkle grew less forbidding in her presence. She radiated what is known today as 'glamour'; but with complete unawareness and indifference, which added to the attraction. Yet, natural and spontaneous though she seemed to be, she had an immense reserve which few, if any, of her companions ever succeeded in penetrating, and when she left the school I doubt if she felt a single pang. She walked away on her last day as casually as though she would be back on the morrow.

For me it was as if a light had been extinguished. Eight years her junior, and far behind in development, I was yet her sister.

But however frustrated and hurt I felt at school, no sooner had I reached home than my heart would grow light again. My tree, my books, the whole warm atmosphere would close about me with welcoming, sheltering grace, and I would feel the relief that for the remainder of the day I should be free from alien personalities and the strain of pursuing a quest I could not attain.

Miss Bunkle was an Englishwoman, and at the time I joined her school she must have been in her early forties. She was tall and angular, with an inflexible figure and a flat, rigid face disfigured by pock-marks. She wore gold spectacles, had very dry colourless lips, and frizzed neutral-tinted hair which she confined in a net. She dressed with a neat severity which gave the impression that she was wearing a uniform.

Beyond coaching the few senior girls who intended to sit for examinations, Miss Bunkle did none of the teaching. That was left to five or six young women, none of whom had ever left the island and whose education had not passed beyond matriculation standard. They all looked anaemic and exhausted, and were drawn from homes where children were numerous and means limited, so that they were thankful to receive the pittance Miss Bunkle paid them. They had little idea of teaching, none at all of maintaining discipline, and only a wholesome dread of Miss Bunkle to qualify them for their posts.

Most of the shortcomings of her establishment were due to the fact that she was too parsimonious to engage even one properly trained mistress; the result was that only the few girls who wished to learn did so, and only the few who came from well-regulated homes gave any order or tone.

One glance from Miss Bunkle's bleak grey eyes glinting behind her spectacles as she stalked through the classrooms, which was her frequent and disconcerting habit, made her assistants tremble. But though she could cow them, it was a different matter when it came to dealing with fifty or sixty spoilt and unruly girls. She could not employ the usual penalties, for this would have resulted in the indignant parents instantly removing their child from the school. Miss Bunkle, therefore, could only maintain order by the sheer force of her personality.

When Ruth had first gone to the school Miss Bunkle's pupils had all been drawn from the same social circle – where in general their mothers knew each other and the children were invited to each other's parties. But by the time she left – some six months after I first went there – Miss Bunkle had begun to enlarge the school and to take girls from many different backgrounds – indeed any whose parents could afford her fees. There were now Portuguese, Venezuelan, Lebanese, Syrian and Greek girls as well as English and French; and some of them to my innocent eyes were odiously precocious. At the age of ten their figures were already ripening, and a year or two later they were powdering their faces and drawing in their waists with corsets. They formed passionate attachments, and, during the recess, took to disappearing from sight in couples with their arms about each other, and only reappeared when the warning bell signalled the return to class.

One of these girls, whose name was Mina, was the daughter of a wealthy Portuguese and she arrived at school each morning in a smart carriage, heavily adorned with jewellery and wearing a silk frock. She was darkly pretty and had long black curls. One day she spoke to me, and a day or two later seated herself beside me during the recess and produced a silver thimble, saying:

'See if it fits you; it's too small for me.' She placed it on my finger. 'Why it fits you beautifully! Keep it.'

'Oh, I couldn't!' I exclaimed.

'Oh, but you *must*!' she urged. 'I like you. I want you for my friend.'

Overcome by shyness and a curious distaste for her, I put the thimble in her lap. Her face flushed angrily.

'All right, don't have it if you don't want it – I don't care!'

I felt decidedly uncomfortable and wished that she would go, but in a moment or two she was smiling once more and telling me that her twelfth birthday was the following week, and that she was having a large party and her father was giving her a gold locket and chain.

'I'm going to put a piece of hair into it – the hair of the person I love best. If you let me love you I'll put your hair in it!'

Suddenly she slipped an arm around me and kissed me on the mouth. I went hot and cold. I was horrified and oddly revolted, but had not the courage to move.

'Don't you like that?' she asked, her face close to mine, her arm pressing me to her. 'Don't you like being kissed?'

'No I don't!' I cried. 'Do let me go'.

To my vast relief at that moment the warning bell rang. Mina stamped her foot angrily, but I jumped up and started to run towards the class. She came after me calling:

'I'll wait for you here tomorrow. I'll bring you a lovely present . . .'

I did not hear what else she said for I could run much faster than she.

The incident haunted me for the rest of the day and I dreaded going to school next morning. I wanted to go and ask my mother to take me away from it, but she would want to know why, and what reason could I give? If I said that a girl had kissed me and I had not liked it she would merely regard it as another example of my 'fastidiousness'. However, the matter was settled for me that very next day without any exertion on my part.

On our arrival at school each morning, as soon as the bell sounded we would arrange ourselves according to classes in a double line on the verandah. One of the mistresses would sit down at the piano and pound out the chords of a march. We marked time with our feet. Then when Miss Bunkle appeared the music would cease. She would incline her head in response to our greeting, murmur 'Good morning, girls', survey our ranks, and then, unless she had any announcements to make, say 'Proceed to your classes', and, as the piano struck up again, we would march off, in somewhat ragged formation, to our various class-rooms.

But on this particular morning, instead of Miss Bunkle the senior mistress appeared. Her face was haggard, and her lips twitched so much that they were scarcely able to frame the words of the usual greeting. I wondered in a frightened way whether Miss Bunkle was dead. Then I saw furtive glances being exchanged between some of the girls: I saw Mina toss her head defiantly, and Freda, a German girl, stick out the tip of her tongue.

Giving a nervous cough the mistress braced herself visibly and said:

'Miss Bunkle has something that she wishes to say to you girls. She wishes to do so in private. During the morning I shall fetch you in to see her one by one. There will be no recess. You can now go to your classes.'

Naturally an acute state of tension brooded over our class. We were all frightened and wondered what had happened. Through the door leading to the next room we could glimpse girls being shepherded away one by one at intervals. The morning was nearly half over when the senior mistress entered our room. It was one of the rare occasions when I happened to be temporarily head of the class, and she called my name. I stood up, the blood rushing into my cheeks and every eye became fixed upon me. She led the way through the main room, every eye following us.

It was the middle of the dry season and I remember noticing how hot and harsh the air was as we emerged on to the front verandah at the end of which was Miss Bunkle's office. The dust lay white on the parched grass of the playground. I noticed a large spider's web spun between two potted palms. Several flies and a silvery moth were entangled in it, and the spider was busily engaged in weaving a neat shroud about the still struggling moth. I longed to free it, while the thought occurred to me how strange it was that, when the mind was turned inward under the influence of some anxiety or apprehension, something so small and insignificant, and quite outside it, could make involuntarily so deep and vivid an impression.

Miss Bunkle was sitting behind a large desk on which ledgers and papers were stacked. Her face was grim and the pock-marks livid. She nodded in dismissal of the mistress and directed me with a gesture to stand in front of her. For what seemed a prodigious time she regarded me in silence. The Venetian blinds were down over the windows, but the glare penetrating between the slats banded everything in gold and sable. At last Miss Bunkle spoke:

'Who are your friends among the girls?'

Shamefacedly I confessed that I had none.

'What? No friends?' she exclaimed incredulously. 'Then who do you play with in the recess?'

'Nobody . . . anybody,' I replied bewildered.

'You must have some particular friend, surely?'

I shook my head and admitted that I often wished I had. Miss Bunkle's spectacles seemed focussed upon me, as though I were a microbe under a microscope, but her next question was so startling that I stared back into them in sheer amazement.

'Do you ever go to the lavatory with other girls?'

As soon as I had absorbed the import of this, the idea filled me with such disgust that I cried out in shocked, indignant tones:

'*Of course not!*'

Miss Bunkle's rigidity relaxed as much as her bony tissue permitted and a sudden brief smile of pure relief lifted the corners of her dry lips. She nodded her head, as though congratulating herself upon something, and said with another smile:

'You may return to your class, collect your books and then go home. Please tell your mother that I have given you a half-holiday.'

I left her in a daze. In a daze I collected my books and strapped them into my satchel, heedless of the many eyes staring at me or the other girl I passed being led to Miss Bunkle's office. Then, as I put the strap of the satchel over my head and got my hat from the back verandah, I quite suddenly came out of my daze and felt vastly relieved and happy, as though a smothering and unclean cloth, which had lain upon my face, had whisked away. I felt as light as air as I ran down the steps and out into the compound. There, in the heavy shade of the mango tree, I saw Matilda, the sweetmeat vendor, sitting behind her tray. Feeling for the forgotten penny in my pocket I went up to her.

Matilda was something of a celebrity: a beloved and familiar figure to several generations of school-children. Her confectionery was famous, and her tiny cottage in Marli Street, where she made it, was patronised by old and young alike. She sold 'tuck' during the recess at our school and at the Queen's Royal College besides, and at both her coming was looked forward to as the great event of the morning.

'E-e-h, darlin', which part yo' is gwine?' she asked.

Torn this way and that by small agonies of indecision as I gazed down at the array of cakes and sweetmeats on her tray I said briefly that I had been given a half-holiday.

'Dat be good,' she said, and, as I selected a sugar-cake and handed her the penny, she gathered up some roasted peanuts in her fingers and put them in my pocket, saying 'Here be li'l lagniappe fo' yo'.'

I had thanked her and was making for the gate when she brought me to a stop by asking:

'Why yo' is not waitin' fo' de odder chillum to walk home wid yo'?'

I had forgotten about that – and so it would seem had Miss Bunkle.

'No,' I replied. 'I don't mind going alone.'

'It aint right,' she said. 'Yo' mudder gwine be well vex'. An' I hear people is sayin' dey's be landin' cattle dis mornin'. Watch out fo' sure.'

At that I felt a spasm of fear. Cattle were imported from Venezuela, and there being in those days no dock facilities for landing them, they were simply swum ashore from the cattle-boats. Not infrequently the animals, herded on board half-wild from the savannahs, maddened by confinement, heat, hunger and thirst, and driven more frantic still by the yelling of the drovers, stampeded on reaching land and spread panic throughout the town. Timid people dreaded the days cattle were landed and stayed at home behind locked gates. I should have to walk practically the entire length of Tranquillity Avenue alone. I felt my courage oozing away. But better go than wait, perhaps for an hour or more, for someone to accompany me.

My courage returned as I reached the gate and saw the road before me empty and silent except for a tram on its clattering way to town. Tall trees bordered the unpaved sidewalk, up through which their roots bulged. Their shade, and that of the high wall on my other hand, mitigated the heat, and as I walked I ate the peanuts, dropping their shells and pretending I was an explorer in a jungle making a trail to guide me back to my camp.

Suddenly the drowsing peace was shattered. Pandemonium broke out behind me. I stopped aghast, and looked back, and my heart seemed to rocket out of my breast. Down the middle of the road was careering a black bull, its hooves thundering: foam flew from its mouth and nostrils, and its breathing was an audible roar as it charged towards me. A crowd of men were vainly pursuing it. Some flourished long sticks, one waved a lasso, another rang a warning bell, and all shouted at the tops of their voices: 'Mad bull! Mad bull! Run! Run! Run!'

I ran with all the speed I possessed. The heat was reverberating up from the blinding white road. The sweat soaked me, hot and cold in turns. My satchel bumped against my leg and hampered me, but I never thought of dropping it. Terror urged me on with every ounce of strength that was in me. The pounding of the hooves, the clangour of the bell, the shouting of the drovers merged into the frantic hammering of my own heart. My knees were failing, my strength spent: I could hardly see, for my eyes were blinded with sweat, terror and exhaustion.

I had passed the high wall and reached a row of small bungalows set back from the sidewalk behind wooden palings. Their gates usually stood open, but today they were shut. The bull was close behind me now; there was a red-hot band of pain around my chest; my breath came in gasping sobs. I knew I could go no further; I stumbled over a tree-root, and as I came down I felt my arm seized.

The next thing I knew I was lying on a sofa in the sitting-room of one of the bungalows while a woman sponged my face. She had seen my plight and, rushing to her gate, had dragged me in from under the very horns and hooves of the bull . . .

I do not know which influenced my parents more: the 'irregularities' at Miss Bunkle's, or the dangers to which she had so thoughtlessly exposed me by allowing me to walk home alone.

Whichever it was I never returned to the school. Arrangements were made for me to have private tuition, and yet another stage in my erratic education began.

CHAPTER THIRTEEN

Plantation Visits

Writing of plantation life in the West Indies, Arthur Knapp said in a book published many years ago: *

There is a fiction, but I think it is true, that very few, if any, who become planters in the tropics ever return permanently to England. The hospitality of the planters is proverbial: there must be something good and free about a planter's life to produce men so genial and generous.

The general truth of this is something to which I can testify. For while tyrannical cruelty and abuse of power could be found on some estates – particularly large sugar estates where there was an absentee owner – yet more commonly the picture was of kindly, perhaps less prosperous, proprietors or managers who lived on their land and whose relations with their employees were cordial and warm. Such were the men I remember, for they were my parents' friends. As for their hospitality: English, Scottish or French, as a visitor you were received into the very hearts of their households; you were welcomed as though your arrival at the plantation was the one thing all were awaiting to complete their happiness; all they possessed was laid before you. The whole aura of the place was friendly, warmed through with geniality. No matter how full the house might be there was always room to put up another bed, and room at the table for another guest. You

---

* *Cocoa & Chocolate: their History from Plantation to Consumer*, Chapman & Hall Ltd, London.

expanded under the influence of such a welcome. All that was required of you was to be happy and enjoy yourself.

Such a household was that of my great-uncle, Maurice Rostant, at Santa Cruz.

Santa Cruz lies in a valley within carriage distance of Port-of-Spain, from which we would set out for the day while the morning was still cool. The road wound through some of the most beautiful scenery in the island – or, indeed, of anywhere in the tropics. Spreading trees and giant clumps of bamboos arched overhead; rivulets ran beside the road among dark cocoa plantations where the air was moist and sweet, heavy with the fragrance of cocoa-lilies and where the cocoa-pods made glowing splashes of crimson and orange among the prevailing green. The whole country was lush and fertile, and the heights above were clad in virgin forest: a tangle of tall, slender trees and luxuriant undergrowth linked by festoons of creeper, a wealth of green, infinite and varied. The beauty of it all was mysterious and haunting.

Uncle Maurice's house was large and rambling, built and furnished for use rather than beauty, and raised high above the ground on pillars. Everything in it was shabby from long use, and it stood in a large untidy garden in the midst of the cocoa trees, through which a stream wound its way, flowing over a bed of pure white sand, and here and there cascading between great purple-black boulders and forming deep pools.

The mode of life here was very different from that at Piedmont. My grandfather had merely changed his domicile from England to Trinidad. The methodical routine of his house at San Fernando followed as nearly as possible that of a similar establishment in the land of his birth. Uncle Maurice on the other hand had been born in the island. He held to the French traditions, but his roots were set deep in the soil of Trinidad and had not merely been transplanted from France. His wife and his wife's people also had their roots in that selfsame soil. When they spoke of 'home' they meant Trinidad. When my grandfather spoke of 'home' he meant England.

Uncle Maurice's household was typical of French-Creole family life. When one visited Santa Cruz one did not merely visit Uncle Maurice, his wife and family; one visited a considerable section of the clan, for the house was always filled with relations of all ages, from ancient crones to infants in arms. Some might be only spending a day, others were on a more protracted visit, while not a few lived there altogether.

Uncle Maurice's wife was always addressed as 'Tantan'; the other old ladies were called 'Tantan Charlotte', 'Tantan Louise', and so on. Clad in flowing gowns, spotlessly clean and fresh, their hair swept back into buns, their serene faces lightly powdered, they spent their days in rocking chairs on a spacious side verandah. They never went beyond the house except on Sundays, when they drove to Mass, *en masse*, or on the occasion of a wedding or funeral, when they attended, no matter which it was, garbed from head to foot in black. Their manner was calm and dignified, and they exuded the fragrance of tonka beans, which they kept among their clothes and in their powder-boxes.

The younger women wore crisp muslin frocks, with the befrilled skirts that were then in fashion, drawn into their tiny waists with a satin ribbon. They were generally extremely pretty and had an air of civilised elegance. All had small, high-arched feet, delicate ankles and slender legs. Young and old alike were beautifully shod. The older women shared intimately in the lives of the younger ones, who treated them with a blending of affection and deference; and there was none of that bickering which such a concourse of inter-related women of all ages would provoke in circumstances where the sacrosanctity of the family was less firmly established.

From bedrooms, each of which opened into another – for they had been added to the original house as the need for them arose, and which all gave on to the verandah on which the old ladies sat – came the sounds of nurses bathing and feeding babies or rocking them to sleep, and the pattering of children's bare feet. These were the grandchildren, even great-grandchildren, the children of nephews and nieces, the descendants of uncles, aunts, and cousins.

Uncle Maurice and the men gathered on the front verandah. He was always clad in white, and his thick white hair, which he wore a trifle long, was combed away from his face in a manner which contrived to give him a well-groomed appearance, though except when strangers were present, he seldom wore a jacket until the evening. He always looked fresh and clean, was closely shaven except for a bushy white moustache, and smelled of eau-de-Cologne. He was tall, with an ample, well-fed figure and wobbly stomach, had a deep friendly voice and a humorous twinkle in his dark eyes. He radiated a cheerful, warm-hearted contentment towards life, an easy-going detachment. In his rocker on the front verandah he remained unperturbed by the human tides which ebbed and flowed in the remainder of the house. Their ripples reached, but never engulfed him.

When we arrived at his house Uncle Maurice would kiss my mother on both cheeks, then clasp my father's hand in one of his, while with the other he clapped him on the shoulder.

'*Comment ça va*, Alice? Lechmere, you look so splendid there is no need to ask. It is a treat to see you both!'

Then his voice would soften as he bent down: 'Ah! Here is my little cabbage!' And he would kiss me on the forehead, pat my hand between his own, and say with a merry twinkle: 'And are you going to fall into the river today?' which referred to an incident about which he never failed to chaff me, for when I had been much smaller I had deliberately tumbled into the stream hoping to delay our departure for a while, at least until my clothes had been dried – which shows how much I loved visiting him. However, I had been unceremoniously wrapped in a shawl and bundled into the carriage.

While my father sat with Uncle Maurice on the front verandah, Tantan would lead my mother into her bedroom on the other side of the house to remove her hat and gloves, before conducting her to the group of other Tantans on the side verandah. All these old ladies would rise to greet her and she would be kissed by each in turn amid murmurs of: 'Alice, it is such happiness to see you!'

Then the younger women would come forward to give the respectful dip at the knee which French courtesy demanded, before being kissed by her. Then babies would be displayed and caressed; toddlers have their curls praised, resemblances noted, or a tooth exhibited. Then at last there was a settling down into rockers and inquiries would begin about the wellbeing of absent members of both families, and a general exchange of news, first on my mother's side as she was the visitor, then on theirs. There would be a shaking of heads over some backsliding; a fluttering of hands over a betrothal; pleased smiles at the pregnancy of a recent bride; chuckles at some absurdity, disconsolate shrugs over a misfortune; a dabbing of eyes over the details of a death-bed.

I would be left in the charge of some of the older children. I might regard them somewhat shyly at first, but they would soon get me to replace my frock with a pinafore, remove my shoes and socks, and away we would scamper to the stream, to clamber among the rocks, or to strip and dive and swim in its sunlit waters.

Meanwhile there would be great activity in the kitchen, where the cook and her assistants were preparing the midday feast, while other servants scurried about in the dining-room laying the vast mahogany table. There was a clatter of crockery and a clinking of silver. They chattered and called to each other and giggled over small mishaps. Occasionally Tantan, or one of the younger women, would drift in to see that all was being properly done, or to administer a mild rebuke – '*Doucement, doucement, s'il vous plaît*' – or to call to Cook to inquire if everything was going well. The whole atmosphere was one of informality, and of convivial though spasmodic bustle.

As the hour of noon drew near such sons, sons-in-law, nephews and other male relatives, as had been out about their various jobs on the plantation, would arrive and gather round Uncle Maurice, while José, the elderly butler, offered rum punches and cigars. The talk would be of crops and prices, of buyers' profits and shipments; of labour problems; of overseers, good, bad and indifferent: a world apart from my father's usual one, but a world in which he took more than a superficial interest – as we were soon to discover. Some of the men were sure to have brought specimens of one kind or another for him to identify, and his opinion would be sought on a host of subjects: did he think that deforestation affected rainfall? What about the theory that plant growth was affected by the phases of the moon, as the negroes averred? Was there a future for rubber – it was rumoured that the Government was going to form an experimental plantation? And this new substance, petroleum, of which he had found the first indications on the island, near San Fernando and elsewhere – did he think it would have any commercial value?

Now the clanging of the bell was summoning us children in to lunch, and at the same time Tantan would be sending a message to warn Uncle Maurice that 'breakfast' would be ready in a quarter of an hour; and the latter, disregarding protests, would tell José to serve a final round of punches. Tantan would instantly appear saying in a determined voice:

'Maurice! I will not have breakfast kept waiting by one moment! It is not fair to Cook, and I'm sure Lechmere and Alice are famished!'

Uncle Maurice would give an immense wink to the men and reply soothingly:

'Do not distress yourself, Tantan. Have you ever known me to be late?'

We children would troop in and seat ourselves at a separate table. The toddlers would be lifted on to their high chairs, their nurses crouched at their sides to feed them. Tantan would give the big table a severe scrutiny, set a fork precisely straight here and there, and after obtaining from Cook the assurance that everything was ready, would herself strike a little brass gong.

Before he seated himself Uncle Maurice would come to our table, pinch an ear here, tug a pigtail there, and ask:

'Well, my children, have you all you desire? Is that chicken *fricassé* nice? Eat plenty and grow strong!'

As he pulled out his chair he would move one of the silver dishes of olives from the centre of the table near to my mother's plate, and another to my father's observing with a comfortable laugh:

'Ah-ha! Fingers have been at these olives! Or is Tantan economising?'

Such an idea provoked hearty laughter, while the younger ladies who had indeed helped themselves to olives each time they drifted in and out looked confused.

Tantan protested plaintively:

'I looked at the table myself before I struck the gong and I never noticed! You girls are thoroughly naughty to put me to shame like this!'

More olives were hurriedly brought; Uncle Maurice turned in his chair and asked:

'Have you children been robbed too? Have you been given any wine?'

While course succeeded course and the wines circulated, a hubbub of praise would be poured on Tantan:

'My dear, this *langouste* is delicious!'

Tantan, smiling and nodding her head, agreed as with a piece of bread she settled the last mouthful carefully on her fork.

'It is good – but, *ma chère*, reserve your appetite for the venison that is coming. Maurice himself shot the creature, and he has selected a Chambertin to go with it which I think you like, Lechmere. And Alice, I have ordered *meringues à la Tantan* as the sweet – for you!'

'Tantan, you spoil us!'

These meringues, as their name signified, were a creation of Tantan's own: after they had been baked they were stuffed with a filling made of cream beaten up with old rum, a pinch of grated lemon-rind, and nutmeg.

My father would be pressed and tempted to each delicacy.

'What, Lechmere, you are refusing the *salmé* of morocoy (land-turtle) liver? *Impossible!* You can't disappoint us like this! For three years I have had that creature fattening! Come, come – just a *soupçon* – it melts in the mouth.'

In this atmosphere of subtle flattery which beset him on every side, my father would begin to shed his normal reserve: his eyes twinkled, he chuckled and laughed, and he paid compliments to the ladies. He would be sure to have twinges of gout later on and vow that the next time he went to Maurice's he would be more abstemious; but when the next time came these good intentions would always be discarded as soon as he began to enjoy himself.

Sometimes the conversation at table would turn to Uncle Maurice's and my mother's relations, and then I would prick up my ears. It seemed that half the French families in Trinidad were my cousins, even people I did not know, while there were endless further connections in France with whom a sporadic correspondence was maintained.

To Uncle Maurice the French Revolution had happened

only yesterday, and he never tired of telling about the many branches of the Rostant family: there were Rostans, Rostangs, Rostaings, Rostants, and Rostands. There were troubadours, poets, writers, inventors, courtiers, bishops, dukes, marquises, counts and barons – and even a saint. At various times they had been prominent in France and Piedmont; in Provence when ruled by its Counts; in the principality of Orange and in the Papal States of Avignon and the Comtat Venaissin.

My head would reel as I tried to imagine what a troubadour might be, or to conceive of the Courts of Love in far away Provence, long, long ago. It was so exciting . . . yet also vaguely unsatisfactory to dream about the past. I want to be an ancestor myself, not a descendant, I remember thinking; and I think the same today.

Women had been idealised in those Courts of Love, but what they had *done* was never mentioned, and this also disturbed me. My father's grandmother, Sarah Guppy, had taken out patents for making suspension bridges, and for strange devices like a kettle which boiled eggs while it made tea. She had written childrens' books and helped design a special nail for fixing copper to ships' bottoms. My grandmother Amelia had painted beautiful pictures – like my cousin Theodora – and had made a voyage alone up the Orinoco river. They had been admired for their achievements and I wanted to be like them.

After lunch the entire party would adjourn to the front verandah for strong black coffee, of which cup after cup was drunk while Uncle Maurice quoted Talleyrand's dictum:

> *Noir comme le diable*
> *Chaud comme l'enfer*
> *Pur comme un ange,*
> *Doux comme l'amour.*

The girls would all gather round my father and his mellow mood would expand still further under the stimulus of their lambent glances, their pleasant chatter, their innocent femininity.

As we drove home in the cool of the day, after the siesta,

with the chorus of leave-takings still in our ears, he would murmur pensively:

'Jeanne is growing very pretty – she must be seventeen now . . . Lucille is really remarkably attractive . . . and Clotilde is so dainty – and very interested in geology too: she asked if she might come and see my foraminifera one day.'

My mother, who delighted at this praise of her relations would say mischievously, 'Oh yes, I saw you flirting with all those girls!'

'Flirting indeed!' he would retort, discomfited for the instant. 'What nonsense you talk, Alice.' Nevertheless he would stroke his beard with a pleased and pensive air: 'A most enjoyable day,' would be his final verdict as we entered our house and the carriage drove away.

Woodbrook was the very last of the sugar estates within the boundaries of Port-of-Spain to withstand the city's expansion. Its extensive canefields, which ran down to meet the waters of the Gulf of Paria on a wide beach, were long ago obliterated by the suburb which is known by its name. But in my childhood the place still survived and was carried on in the traditional fashion. Unlike most of the sugar estates today it was privately owned and it possessed its own *usine*, or factory. All grades of sugar except the most refined were produced there.

Its manager was a Scotsman named Watson who had been in charge for a number of years. Its large wooden bungalow had become his home, and its canefields were as dear to him as though they had been his own property. He was a stout man with a Scots accent, bright blue eyes, brown hair and a very red face. Boisterous, warm-hearted, generous and always cheerful, he was generally known as 'Dawson' because of his partiality for Dawson's Perfection Whisky, a popular brand in those days. He was the estate's last manager.

He had married, when he was nearly forty, a cousin of my mother's who was then seventeen, and at the time of which I write they had a son called Ozzie who was three years old. Nini Watson was adorably pretty, with dark eyes and a mass of golden-brown curls, while a pair of deep dimples gave a ravishing quality to her smile. Where her husband was distinctly rough-hewn she was so elegant and dainty that it seemed hardly possible that they would be happily mated. Yet they were. She twisted the burly, red-faced Scotsman round her little finger, and he was passionately and devotedly in love with her.

Hospitality at Woodbrook was on as lavish a scale as at Uncle Maurice's, and the estate was renowned for its Pepper-Pot – a traditional dish of the Caribbean, in which a stew is kept going for year after year by adding to it a preparation of the poisonous juices of the bitter cassava, known as *cassareep*, which has preservative properties. In bygone days, when few roads linked the outlying districts, and these were scarcely more than tracks which the onset of the rains made into quagmires; when the crazy wooden bridges which spanned the numerous streams and mountain rills were liable to be swept away or to collapse for want of repair; when horses and mules formed the only means of transport, and planters might be called upon to provide food for stranded travellers and other unexpected guests; when establishments were large and there were many mouths to feed, and refrigeration was still undreamed of: then the Pepper-Pot was an essential part of every plantation home. Indeed they were objects of great pride in those households which still possessed them and, continuing from generation to generation, frequently achieved more than local renown. The Woodbrook Pepper-Pot was reputed to be a hundred years old, but it was easily outdone by that at Diamond Sugar Estate in British Guiana, which even in those days were claimed to be nearing its second century.

Blackened with age and wrapped around with a napkin, the Woodbrook *canaree* (a huge earthenware pot in which the Pepper-Pot was made and kept) would be placed each day at luncheon on the enormous mahogany sideboard which was a feature of every plantation house. One helped oneself with a wooden spoon, bringing out from the savoury depths a delicious miscellany, and piling it onto rice steamed so that each grain stood out separately.

Many are the stories told of Pepper-Pots. An Englishman visiting Trinidad once told me that he went cold with horror when he suddenly found himself contemplating a tiny clenched fist upon his plate, and was only slightly soothed when it was explained to him that a certain kind of monkey was often eaten in the West Indies.

A famous story relates to a West Indian judge who, declaiming on the wonders of the Pepper-Pot to some impressionable English guests, plunged in the spoon with a flourish, only to extract a ghastly bedraggled object at which he goggled in dismay. The butler, equally aghast, provided the clue.

'Eh-eh! Look at dat now! Dat be Miss Margie's poo' l'il cat! It be two days now since he be lost. How he manage to git in dere at-all?'

When 'crop' was on – as the sugar-cane harvest was called – I would frequently ride my donkey over to Woodbrook to spend the day. After I had played with Ozzie one of the young Scots overseers would mount me on a mule and I would ride with him into the canefields. Under the dazzling sun lines of coolies would be working, cutting and topping each 6 foot tall stem of cane with two quick, successive strokes of the machete, then casting it onto a heap to be loaded later on to huge two-wheeled carts. These were drawn by a yoke of water-buffaloes, animals reputedly always dangerous to Europeans, but docile in the hands of the coolies, even allowing the coolie children to ride on their backs with impunity.

Along the rutted tracks which intersected the canefields these carts moved slowly in single file, their wheels *keening* (creaking) – it was said that the buffaloes would not draw the carts unless the wheels keened – to the *usine*, where the canes were shot under rollers to be crushed, and where the air was filled with the heavy-sweet smell of the sticky, translucent juice. Night and day throughout 'crop' the furnaces roared and the engines never ceased their steady chugging. In enormous copper vats the juice passed through the various stages of boiling and refining, and from them chutes carried the sugar to coolies holding wide the mouths of sacks into which it cascaded. As each sack was filled other coolies sewed them up and 'toted' them to weighing machines, and thence to the store-houses.

At Woodbrook they used to make 9 inch high cone-shaped

sugar-loaves, or *papelons* as they were called, being *'papelloné'*, or covered in scales i.e. wrapped with layer after layer of dried banana leaves, folded as neatly and closely around them as tobacco leaves in a cigar, tied at the top, and trimmed into a rosette. Each season Mr Watson presented us with a basket of papelons: how dark and rich and succulent they were! And how delicious spread over butter on those crisp little loaves of bread which the baker delivered each morning!

I grew to know most of the coolies at Woodbrook, and would visit the barracks to talk to the women: still in their native dress they would be busy about their cooking, or with lime juice and wood-ash polishing the brass bowls and platters which they had brought with them from India, until they shone like gold. And while the women worked their children played naked on the sun-baked earth.

It was at Woodbrook that I saw a group of children afflicted with the morbid vice of clay-eating: a pathetic sight, with hard, protruding stomachs, stick-like limbs, and wizened faces from which their eyes stared enormously with the blank look of the doomed – for few of them survived for long. They turned away from the wholesome food provided for them, and would starve themselves to death in their passion for clay. Nini Watson was trying to cure them, and to prevent them from imparting the habit to others. But she was only successful with one little girl, who became Ozzie's playmate for the brief span of his life – for Ozzie and his mother both died within a few hours of each other of typhoid fever while he was still short of his fifth birthday, and she was hardly more than twenty-five.

With their deaths the life of Woodbrook also came to an end, for Nini's husband could endure the place no longer. He returned in grief and desolation to his native Scotland – whereupon the owner sold the whole estate to speculative builders; the house and *usine* were demolished, and the canefields tilled no more.

CHAPTER FOURTEEN

Down the Islands

In ages long ago Trinidad was united with the mainland of South America, and the mountain range which dominates its northern part was continuous with the coastal cordillera of present-day Venezuela. At some geological epoch a land subsidence had cut off Trinidad, submerging all but certain peaks and ridges which still project above the water in a number of small islands, between which straits known as the Bocas ('Mouths', in Spanish) unite the Gulf of Paria with the Atlantic Ocean. These islands are not only very beautiful, but make ideal places for spending a holiday, and in my childhood 'going down the islands' was a thing to be looked forward to with eager anticipation.

The journey was accomplished in those days in a small paddle-wheeled steamer called the *Ant*. She was slow, she tossed and wallowed, her paddle-wheels groaned and laboured as they churned the waters of the Gulf: the grown-ups complained that she was insufferably hot and reeked of oil; but to children every moment on board was an unqualified delight, and the *Ant* was a magic argosy bearing them to a veritable paradise.

Her first port of call was a group of islets just beyond the fringe of the harbour, known as the Five Islands. They clustered closely together each crowned by a bungalow, the gay red and white striped roof of which could be glimpsed between embowering trees. After discharging passengers and freight into the row-boats which came out to meet her, the *Ant* laboured on to a couple of larger islands, and afterwards to the three largest of all: Gasparee (Gasparile), Monos* and Chacachacare.**

The Five Islands and Gasparee were rocky and had few beaches, and for this reason we seldom went to them; but the shores of Monos and Chacachacare were fretted into numerous sandy bays, girt by rocky arms over which the sea broke in glittering spray, and sheltered by lofty wooded peaks rising steeply behind them. These bays were privately owned, each with a house upon it which the owner was prepared to let or lend when he did not need it himself.

My father enjoyed a holiday 'down the islands' as much as we did, but my mother was less enthusiastic. Certainly she enjoyed the opportunity it gave her of gathering family and friends together under one roof; and she beamed with pleasure at beholding everyone eating and drinking, with appetites made keen by sea-air and exercise, the fare which she had taken infinite forethought to provide. But she had no real taste for an al-fresco existence. She did not enjoy sea-bathing and was nervous in a boat, so that at the end of our stay, which sometimes lasted as long as four weeks, while we others were sadly contemplating leaving, she would be looking forward to a return to urban amenities with great contentment.

During the days of preparation for such a holiday our household was agog with excitement. I, needless to say, skipped about with untiring zest, poking my nose into all that was going on, and taking particular interest in the paraphernalia which my father was busy getting ready in the study. There were killing bottles for rare insects which might fly in at night attracted by the lamp-light; setting boards and long setting pins as fine as hairs; a butterfly net, and a dredging net on a long pole for scooping up marine specimens; *flambeaux* to attract fish at night; a geological hammer; various buckets, and a glass tank in which to keep specimens alive until drawings had been made of them; dissecting instruments and

---

* *Monos* (Sp.) – Monkey, so called because of the Red Howler monkeys that lived there, and which would come down to the beach each evening.
** *Chacachacare* – An onomatopoeic Carib word derived from the rattling of dry seeds in the pods of certain beans when the plant is shaken by the wind.

bottles of preserving spirit; fishing lines of various thickness with hooks of various sizes; and finally the microscope which my father permitted no-one but himself to touch.

With an air which grew more and more distracted as the date of our departure drew nearer, my mother became immersed in the question of provisions. Orders had to be placed for fresh meat, bread, ice, vegetables, to be despatched to us by the *Ant* on each of her three trips a week. The basic supplies had to go with us. So my mother made lists and lost them, and made them anew. She became obsessed with the fear that some essential would be forgotten – matches? candles? oil for the lamps? . . . She might spring out of bed at night crying 'Vinegar!' and grope frantically for a pencil. In the midst of entertaining a visitor I have seen her lips moving and heard her murmuring under her breath, 'Cucumbers and lard . . . cucumbers and lard' with desperate concentration.

She would hurry suddenly into the study and confront my father with several sheets of paper.

'Lechmere, just glance through these, will you? I feel sure I've forgotten something.'

My father would run his eye over them protesting:

'But, Alice, we go down the islands every year and last year I gave you a book with a standard list of all the essentials, to save you all this bother.'

My mother would make a gesture of distress and apology.

'Yes, dear. I know. You did.'

'Well, where is it?'

'Gone! Vanished! I've hunted for it high and low.'

'Oh, Alice! You know it's perfectly simple to have a proper place for things and keep them in it.'

'Yes . . . I know! I know! . . . I do try – but they never remain there.'

'They don't walk off of their own accord, you know.'

'No, of course not; but the servants move them to dust and forget to put them back – or the children take them . . .'

'But they don't do that with my things.'

'No, indeed . . . but that's quite different somehow.'

Both knew that the difference lay in the fact that while my father was scrupulously methodical my mother was not, but neither said so. Instead, my father would tell her to leave the lists with him and, when she was gone, he would check them with one secretly kept to meet this inevitable emergency.

Early on the morning of our departure a couple of hand-carts would arrive to take our stores and baggage to the quay. On to them were loaded boxes of groceries, baskets of live poultry, a crate with a couple of piglets, a turtle or two lying on their backs; baskets of oranges and limes, several stems of bananas and strings of onions, and, enclosed in bags of saw-dust, two large York hams.

Having learned to swim almost as soon as I could walk I was completely at home in the sea. I got into my bathing trunks at dawn and remained in them until sundown. I was raptur-ously happy on those beaches: my heart sang and I experi-enced that exultation which comes from spiritual release and physical well-being. I loved the sea, the ever-lasting sea, which remains despite man's defiling hand still free, uncon-quered and unchanged.

My father, too, loved it as much as I did. Within sight and sound of it he became as happy as myself. In an old shirt, sea-stained trousers and straw hat, climbing over the rocks, peering into crevices, wading along the shore with his dredg-ing net, one would hear him singing snatches of song.

> *If I had a donkey that wouldn't go*
> *Do you think I would wallop him? No! No! No!*
> *I'd give him some hay and cry Gee — Whoa!*
> *Young lambs to sell, young lambs to sell!*
> *If I'd as much money as I could tell*
> *I never would cry young lambs to sell!*

All he took in the way of specimens went into the buckets, and when the sun grew hot he would sit on the sand in the shade of a wild tropical almond tree and examine his treasure-trove more minutely, putting those he wished to keep into the glass tank and emptying the remainder back into the sea.

We never knew how many guests would be with us at the week-ends, for, over and above those invited by my mother, my brother Jim might sail down in his yacht *Vanessa Io* with a party of anything up to half a dozen. If there were not enough beds, hammocks would be slung along the verandahs; if the long table in the dining-room was not large enough to seat us all, another would be found from somewhere and added to one end.

The keen fishermen would set out before sunrise to troll for tarpon, returning at noon to display their catches – or tell tales of those that got away – as they sipped Planters' punch. After a bathe, rum swizzles preceded lunch which, especially on Sundays, was a feast indeed. The whole atmosphere was convivial, intimate and carefree.

Oh happy, happy days!

Each evening a night-line was baited, one end being made fast to the jetty with a bell attached to it, and the hook rowed out to sea and cast overboard. At any moment of the night the bell might clang, and then out we all dashed in our night attire to haul in the line. One night it set up such clangour that it roused even the boatmen and the caretaker. We hauled in slowly, for the strain on the line was tremendous, and presently a monster shark was threshing the water. After a terrific battle it was dragged ashore, and as we stood in wonder at its size the caretaker slit open its belly revealing a whole family of baby sharks. They wriggled and flapped on the sand. Some the boatmen killed, to salt down and eat; the rest we put into the water to see what they would do. They swam close inshore, and when we went in among them they came nosing against our legs as though seeking protection. They were without fear, and, I think, without sight.

One night I was bitten by a vampire bat. In the morning I could not rouse myself and my mother, coming in search of me, found the sheets and mattress about my feet saturated with blood. Four tiny but deep incisions in the tip of my big toe were the only visible marks of the attack, but for two or three days afterwards I suffered from low fever and was weak from loss of blood.

It was while recovering from this misadventure that I lay one morning in a hammock slung under the wild almond tree listening drowsily to the shrilling of insects and the whisper of the sea upon the sands. The sky was over-patterned with its large leaves, some, russet-gold prior to falling, looking as if they had been cut out of copper with a large knife, the others polished shining green. Across my line of vision there suddenly darted a humming bird. Here and there among the foliage it flashed with iridescent loveliness, hanging poised between each flight, its tiny flame-coloured body quivering with ecstatic life. Then in an instant it vanished as suddenly as a flame blown out by a breath. I could only suppose that I had missed its final swoop.

I do not know how long it was before something fell into my lap. It was all that remained of the humming bird: a dessicated fragment of skin and feathers.

A sudden fury seized me. I was up the tree in a moment, and there confronting me, bloated of belly, was a praying mantis, the largest I have ever seen. It stood as relentlessly erect as an exclamation mark, turning its triangular face to regard me malignantly, while the cruel forelimbs which with such lightning swiftness had seized and killed the humming bird were folded characteristically as though in prayer. I broke off a stout twig and lashed at it. Out shot its forelimbs in defence, and its eyes burned like live coals. Fierce and evil it was – and fearless. It stood up to my blows, but I lashed at it mercilessly until it fell. Then I ran off to fetch my father. It was still twitching when we returned, but the ants were already busy with it.

One of the bays on Monos was called 'Morrison's' after its owner, a Scotsman of that name. He had come to Trinidad many years before as a young man, bought the bay and made his home there. Here Charles Kingsley had visited him and was so fascinated by the life he lived that he wrote in his book *At Last*:

I looked at the natural beauty and repose; at the human vigour and happiness; and I said to myself . . . 'Why do not other people copy this wise Scot? Why should not many young couples, who have education, refinement, resources in themselves . . . retreat to some such paradise as this . . . leaving behind them false civilisation, and vain desires and useless show; and there live in simplicity and content "The Gentle Life?" '

Certainly to me also Mr Morrison's life seemed ideal, and my great desire was that my father should buy a bay and settle down in like manner. He was a tall, handsome old man, tanned a deep mahogany and with a square white beard. With him lived his two daughters, one of whom was the postal agent, while he himself acted as Government superintendent, his principal duty being to see that the pathway which traversed the island from end to end half way up the hillside was kept in order; for the freehold of the bays extended inland only so far as this path, the mountain ridge above being Crown property.

Whenever we were at Monos he would come striding along this path to see my father, and they would indulge in long talks. Often he would regale us with anecdotes of Kingsley, of whom naturally he was a great admirer, and all of whose books he treasured.

The Morrisons kept a quantity of poultry. The ducks took readily to the sea in which they swam happily. They had learned not to put their heads under water or to dibble it through their bills; yet the moment they came upon fresh water they instantly recognised the difference and would dive and dibble energetically.

With one exception the caretakers in charge of the various bays were coloured men. The exception was John Brown, an Englishman. His past was something of a mystery, but it was generally supposed that he had come to Port-of-Spain with a circus, and when it departed had elected to remain behind. Of medium height, he was thin and sun-dried, with sharp features and shrewd, lively blue eyes. His lazy voice, dry humour and carefree contentment all fascinated me, as did his power over animals. Among his many pets was a pelican. Completely tame though with unclipped wings, it lived ashore with him, and whenever he went out fishing it perched on the prow of his boat. Now and then he would toss it a fish, but it made no attempt to take those he threw into the bottom of the boat. Sometimes it would flap off and dive for fish on its own account, but it always returned to its station on the prow, where it brooded solemnly, bill upon chest.

John Brown had several dogs, cats, monkeys, and birds – which flew in and out of his bungalow and fed from his hand.

One he had taught to light a match with its beak, while its foot steadied the box. I often used to run over by the hill path to be entertained by the tales of his adventures, which were innumerable, for he claimed to have travelled all the world over. One day as we sat astride an upturned boat – he was making a new fishing line – he told me of a strange experience.

About the hour of sunrise a few months before he had got out of bed and stood leaning over his verandah rail. There was a pearly mist over the sea which shrouded the jetty so that it was barely visible. Then he became aware that there was a boat drawn up on the beach and a small group of people gathered about it. He could see no sloop or launch from which they could have disembarked, but one might, he thought, be lying out in the bay concealed by the mist. He stared at the group in some annoyance, for he had received no intimation from the owner of the bay to expect visitors; and then with astonishment because they seemed so oddly dressed. All wore what appeared to him to be long black coats reaching to the ground and black hoods over their heads. As he watched they all began to walk slowly inland.

Hurriedly pulling on his clothes he took the keys of the house from the nail on which they hung, and hastened the hundred yards from his bungalow. But the party was nowhere to be seen. He walked round to the back of the house, and up and down the hillside but there was no trace of them; and when, bewildered, he turned back it was to see that the boat from which they had landed had vanished too.

'What d'you make of that, Missy?' he asked me.

'Ghosts?' I suggested, awed.

'Must have been. I've seen a packet of queer things in my time, but it's taken Monos to show me ghosts.'

'Have you ever seen them again?' I asked.

'Not that gathering on the beach; but one evening, up along the Government path, a figure dressed just like that crossed only a few yards in front of me. I called out and went after it, but it just seemed to melt away.'

Then he said that only the previous week, when clearing some bush on a little plateau below the path, he had discovered the crumbling remains of a building. He took me to see

it. It must once have been a fairly large building, but apart
from the broken arch of a doorway obscured by convolvulus
vines, all that remained were the low pillars that had once
supported the floor. It was not an impressive ruin, but there
was about it that melancholy which clings to all ruins, speak-
ing as they do of human endeavour vanquished and human
hopes abandoned: poignant reminders of mortality.

Who had these people been, and where had they gone, and
why?

'See here,' said John Brown, pointing above our heads.
'They planted a grove of orange and shaddock trees up to the
front door.' The trees were infested with parasites and dying.
'And see here again,' and he led me a short distance through
the bush along the narrowing plateau 'see here, this looks like
a burial ground.'

Under the entanglement of lianes and high weeds was
visible a row of mounds which might indeed have been
graves, while the decaying stumps of a hardwood post or two
showed where once a fence had enclosed them.

I did not tell John Brown's story to anyone, even my father.
I felt he would not have wished me to. But I told my father
about the ruins, and asked if he knew anything about them.
But he had no knowledge of any buildings on Monos earlier
than the last twenty or thirty years. Many years afterwards,
however, I learned that an order of nuns had migrated from
Venezuela, though no-one could tell me when, and built a
small convent upon that very site. No-one could say how long
they had stayed there or what had caused them to abandon so
peaceful a retreat. Were the black-habited figures whom John
Brown saw the ghosts of those who had died there, and
whose bones lay in the forgotten graves among the tangled
vegetation which had so quickly and relentlessly obliterated
them and their convent?

Once we were unable to rent a bay on Monos and my father
was offered a place called Todd's Bay on the island of Gasparee. We had been there on visits, and my mother disliked it
intensely. She said that its atmosphere was sinister. The sea
pounded incessantly against the rocks upon which the bungalow was built, undercutting them so that it sucked and

smacked with gruesome gurgles underneath and burst up through blow-holes in sudden fountains. The entire island was honey-combed with caves linked by subterranean waterways. These caves were the haunts of bats and owls, both of which the negroes regarded with superstitious awe; and of the even more dreaded 'jumbie-birds' or oilbirds (*Steatornis caripensis*), so called because of their ghastly, unnerving cries – a 'jumbie' being a ghost.

Immediately in front of the house was a headland which bore the name Pointe Baleine, for the place had once been a whaling station and many of the huge copper vats in which blubber had been boiled down were still to be seen. The sea about this point could be exceedingly rough, and the tides were dangerous, for it faced the narrow First Boca where a bottle-neck of churning water like a tidal bore, and called the *remous*, was formed when the tide was turning. So powerful and treacherous was the *remous* that in those days Lloyds would not accept for insurance any ship which used it.

So when my father announced that he had been offered Todd's Bay my mother was most reluctant to accept. Passengers often had great difficulty in disembarking there into boats from the *Ant*, and there had been occasions when the *Ant* had been unable to land stores for two or three trips in succession.

But my father, who particularly wished to explore the caves, laughed away her fears and overcame her objections. He would charter a sloop, he said, to take us down and bring us back, the water at the landing stage being deep enough to allow a sloop to go alongside, and this would obviate the difficulty of disembarking into boats. As for stores, he went on, we would take emergency rations, although rough seas were unlikely at that time of year. My mother was far from convinced: storms were Acts of God, she murmured, and could assail us at any time; and then, her practical disposition asserting itself, she inquired doubtfully:

'Emergency rations? What sort of emergency rations?'

My father's eyes twinkled as he suggested a barrel of ship's biscuits and a keg of pickled pork.

'*Mon dieu!*' my mother gasped in horror. 'Ship's biscuits and pickled pork! Is *that* what you expect us to live on?'

'Why not?' said my father with the utmost gravity. 'The mariners of old discovered half the world on such fare.'

'But the children! You can't expect the children . . . '

'The children,' my father cut in with conviction, 'would consider it the greatest lark in the world to be marooned on Gasparee and live on a diet of ship's biscuits and pickled pork.'

We went on board the sloop in the early afternoon to get the benefit of the offshore breeze before it dropped at sunset. The piglets squealed, the chickens and ducks and turkeys squawked, quacked and gobbled in their respective crates, as our crew of one man and two boys cast loose and hoisted the sails. My mother sat in a chair on the small aft deck, looking anxious and with a hint of martyrdom in her expression, yet unable to refrain from smiling at the obvious enjoyment of my father and ourselves. He had insisted on bringing the ship's biscuits and pickled pork, and we all made a great joke of these.

Everything went serenely, for the greater part of our stay; then, just before the end, a tempestuous storm broke upon us. The bungalow rocked under its onslaught. It whipped the sea into a turmoil and, as the breakers crashed ceaselessly against the headland, spindrift drenched the house making everything within it dank and odorous. The rain hurled itself upon the galvanised iron roof with so prodigious a noise that one could hardly hear oneself speak. Thunder roared, and lightning tore across the heavens in lurid coruscations. With the passing of one storm another brewed, and all the while the rain and the spindrift met and mingled in a soaking mist. At each first peal of thunder my mother would fling herself on her bed and cover her head with a pillow, and so remain until the storm had passed. But even after the thunderstorms had died away, the sea, the wind and the rain continued with unabated violence. Thrice we watched the *Ant* put about in the distance and return to harbour carrying our supplies with her. The last fowl had been killed, the last loaf of bread eaten; only a few fragments of ham adhered to the bone; only a tin or two of sardines remained in the store; with such a sea running it was impossible to fish. The barrel of ship's biscuits and the keg of pickled pork were broached.

My mother was near to despair, and though my father kept up a cheerful appearance he cast many an anxious look at the sky; and when, day after day, the sloop failed to arrive he too grew worried.

'It's this wretched pickled pork and ship's biscuits of yours that have brought us bad luck,' my mother lamented. 'You tempted Providence.'

'We should have been a good deal more wretched without them,' my father retorted. 'You take a poor view of Providence, I declare!'

But the following day the sloop did come, which was just as well for our last meal consisted of the remains of the biscuits soaked in coffee.

The passage back to Port-of-Spain was exceedingly rough. The servants, flopped in a heap, clung to each other groaning, and praying aloud between paroxysms of sea-sickness. My mother sat with a strained, pallid face and a rigid body, clasping my father's hand except when, with an agonised gesture, she indicated that he was to assist her speedily to the sloop's side. But the wind was with us and the sloop rode the waves magnificently; and the boys, Ruth and I sat in the bows and shouted and cheered as the bowsprit pointed now to the darkling sky when she rose on the crests, now to the green depths as she slid into the troughs.

As my mother stepped shakily ashore she quoth, like Poe's raven: 'Nevermore!'

CHAPTER FIFTEEN

Uprootings

About this time of which I have been writing, my grandfather was taken seriously ill and my father immediately left for San Fernando. An atmosphere of subdued tension closed upon us.

'If he dies,' declared my mother dramatically 'it will be the end of an epoch in our lives.'

And she was right. Soon the news came that there was no hope of recovery, and messengers were despatched post-haste to the shops for crêpe and black materials, and the seamstress hastily summoned. Then we heard that he was dead. The date was November 12, 1894.

He was to be buried at San Fernando beside his wife Amelia and their son, Francis Jeune, and with the necessity for haste which a death in the tropics imposes, a spell of feverish activity ensued. A special train was ordered to convey the mourners, and weeping, my mother prepared herself for the ordeal.

Early in the morning relations and friends gathered at our house. In deepest mourning, with hats and faces swathed in crêpe, they hung about the drawing-room in unnatural attitudes. The jalousies were closed and in the dim light everyone looked ghostly and frightening, while the heavy scent from all the wreaths was overwhelming. I found myself shivering and longing for them to go. Yet when they had driven away in a procession of closed carriages the house seemed as empty as a hollow shell, and the very sunshine drained of colour and warmth.

Feeling wilted and forlorn I watched the servants sweeping and tidying. A tuberose, a crushed and yellowing lily, a mauve orchid were swept away. I wanted to save them and put them in water, but I could not make the effort to do so. I longed to get away by myself, but the urgent need for human contact kept me to the house. The family would not be back until late that night, and left to their own devices the servants gathered idly in the yard and discussed the mourners in strident tones, or vied with each other in describing the details of other funerals they had known until, sickened, I crept away to my tree.

The picture I had retained of old Thorpe lying dead had haunted me at intervals for a long while afterwards and then receded into the background of my mind. Mary Hodge's death had brought it into the foreground again for a time, and once more it had receded. Now it returned with a more compelling clarity and poignancy. It had become the pro-totype of death and of death's finality. Just as there had been no more old Thorpe, so there was no more Mary; and now there was no more Grandpa. Mary Hodge's bungalow still stood where it always had, So, too, would Piedmont. Both I had known intimately and loved. Now death excluded me from them for ever.

I ached with the thought of the mischievous things I had done at Piedmont and of how I had sometimes teased Mary. If only once more I could see Grandpa standing on the steps to welcome us! If only I could say how sorry I was and show him how good I could be . . . If only I could run just once more into the pink bungalow and feel that lovely sense of warmth and elemental rhythm . . . But death had precluded that also. The crushing sense of loss, the pain of regrets pressed down upon me.

The day was interminably long. I felt exhausted, but on being put to bed I could not sleep. When my parents at last tip-toed into my room. I was still awake. I longed to ask if I could stay in their bed.

'Why aren't you asleep?' my mother asked.

'I was listening for you.'

My father bent to kiss me, and his voice sounded flat and tired. I could see how sad and exhausted he was.

'Go to sleep now; we are back and it's after ten o'clock.'
As he left the room my mother asked:
'Have you said your prayers?' I shook my head. 'Then say them now with me.'

When I had been so very young that I cannot recall it, she had taught me to repeat *Ave Maria* at bedtime: and at some slightly later date my father had added the Lord's Prayer with the following verse to close my devotions:

> *When in my little bed I lie,*
> *Heavenly Father, hear my cry;*
> *Lord, protect me through the night*
> *And bring me safe to morning light.*

As I reached this point now, my mother told me to add: 'May Grandpa rest in peace. Amen.' I felt consoled by that and after she had gone I whispered: 'And old Thorpe and Mary Hodge too.'

Soon after this another event was to take place which would change the tenor of our lives even more: All Saints' Rectory was next door to us, and the church just beyond. The incumbent all these years had been an old man of studious habits and quiet disposition; but now he was succeeded by another who had a large family of boys, was an enthusiast for bell-ringing, and kept a flock of guinea-fowl. The clamour of the boys, the pealing of the bells and the screeching of the guinea-fowl reiterating their everlasting demand to *Come-back! Come-back!* were too much for my father. Always acutely sensitive to noise, he was driven to distraction by the pandemonium. He still owned and edited the *Almanack* at that time, and he found it impossible to concentrate on the intricate calculations involved, so that at last the decision to sell our house was forced upon him. My mother deplored the need, but recognised the necessity.

A new house, which suited the requirements of both my parents, was not easy to find. My mother was reluctant to live elsewhere than 'on the Savannah', but since such houses rarely came into the market, and when they did fetched fabulous prices, she had finally to be content with one which gave her only rather oblique views of it. For my father, however, it possessed an important compensation: the garden provided ample space to add a wing which could contain not only a larger study and workshop, but a tower which he had long wanted to build to house his telescope and facilitate his astronomical observations.

The building operations were at least a distraction from the deep sadness we all felt at leaving the old house we loved. But when the moment of actual departure came I knew that no matter where we lived the rhythm of our life would never be quite so smooth again, and that nothing would ever compensate me for leaving my tree – and nothing did.

I went to bid it good-bye after everyone was gone and the empty house had been locked up. How silent and melancholy it seemed! How abandoned and forlorn was everything around! I can remember my curious sense of fatigue as I pressed my hands and forehead against the tree's rough bark, the sudden sense of despair that came with the realisation of how helpless I was in the face of destiny. It was an agony to think that my tree even now belonged to others who would never love it as it was accustomed to be loved; and that never after this passing hour would I be able to come and find sanctuary close to it. Hunched on its highest root, with my face in my hands, I sat for a long while recalling all that had happened since my eyes had first opened to the knowledge of it; and it seemed to me that only that part of my life which had been lived in the shadow of its branches was real and true. It was my shrine, the holy place of my legend, and all else in my life was fortuitous, extraneous. When at last I got up to go I felt strangely old, and as vulnerable as though I had shed a protecting skin.

I was never to see my tree again, for on the very morrow its new owners cut it down.

Our new house must have been built at much the same time as our old one. Its design was somewhat similar, but its rooms were less spacious, less gracious and lacked the dignity which those of the other possessed. It was closer to the road, too, with a tiled pathway, bordered by rosebeds, leading to the front door. Although the front garden was considerably smaller, the whole compound itself was quite as large, but somehow devoid of charm or character. It had been planned just as a convenient place in which to carry on existence; no loving pride had gone to its creation, to transform it into a home and breathe a soul into it. And so it remained for me: soulless. My mother arranged the furniture and hung up the pictures, but they did not blend into the rooms; they merely furnished them. We occupied it for many years and were contented enough with it, but it never claimed our affection and it never gained the imprint of our personalities.

At first I roved the garden and backyard disconsolately, searching for some niche to call my own. The only large tree was a mango. It was a handsome tree, but it grew near the kitchen and its shade was quickly monopolised by the servants in which to pass their hours of ease. Then on one tour of investigation I discovered that the house was raised high enough from the ground to allow me to stand erect beneath. Exploring further I found that a portion of this space had been enclosed with jalousies, and that access to it was by means of a door which was very effectively concealed by a croton hedge. The former owner had evidently used it as a wine-cellar, but now nobody but myself seemed aware of its existence. It was festooned with cobwebs as thick and black as crêpe, and littered with straw and other debris, but I saw at a glance that it could be transformed into a pleasant enough little room which would afford me the privacy I sought. Carefully I cleaned it out. Next, inveigling some whitewash and an old brush out of Laycock I whitewashed as much of the wall space as I could reach; then, furnishing one corner with doll's house tables and chairs, I installed my 'little people' there, while in the rest of the room two discarded grown-ups' chairs, a table and a square of matting did for me. Thenceforward this little cellar played many parts: sometimes it was a smuggler's cave to which admittance could only be gained by a password; sometimes it was the crypt of Old St. Paul's during the Great Plague, as described by Harrison Ainsworth; and yet again it was the quarterdeck of the *Victory* and I, Nelson – a hero both then and now – pacing it at Trafalgar.

As time went on I further improved its appearance by pasting up coloured plates from illustrated papers, and I made it more comfortable with the aid of a cushion or two, while upon a shelf across one corner I arranged some of my favourite books.

Soon after we moved to our new home the house next door but one was taken by four men whom my mother, possessor of two unmarried daughters – albeit I was still a child – described as 'the most eligible bachelors in the island'. Its joint occupation by these four friends – all of whom had been posted to Trinidad by the Colonial Office – caused it to be known as 'the Chummery'.

Now that I was older I was allowed to ride my donkey in the Savannah with greater freedom, and one afternoon, reining in to watch a cricket match, I found myself next to a thin man on a fat cob whom I recognised as one of the members of the Chummery. He had a narrow face, a rather long, thin nose, a pair of the kindest and most twinkling eyes, and a wide attractive smile. We exchanged greetings. I told him that the name of my donkey was Greycoat and asked him the name of his horse.

'Butter,' he said, 'because he is rather fat!'

His voice and manner were so gentle and friendly that I felt perfectly at ease with him.

Presently I asked him for which of the cricket teams he and his friends were going to play. He looked puzzled, and replied that the only one of them who played cricket was 'A.M.'

'But I heard my mother say you were all such good catches,' I said – and could not understand why he was so amused!

Paddy Jones and I became great friends and often went riding together on Sunday mornings. He invited me to meet the others members of the Chummery, and they made much of me, giving me stamps for my collection and generally spoiling me. But he once gave me a brand new five-shilling piece; and indeed I began to regard him, grown-up though he was, as my best friend.

CHAPTER SIXTEEN

Before the Ball

It was considered essential that a girl, before being launched on Society, should spend at least a year in England, preferably three or four, being 'finished'. There only would she have a chance to eradicate the insidious singsong Creole accent and acquire that poise and complexion, that *cachet*, which would enhance her chances of making a 'good match': which, if she failed to do, would mean that she had failed in the whole object of a woman's existence, and after a season or two would be relegated to the background of the home, there to live parasitically or to eke out a genteel existence in some ladylike way.

It was hardly less important that a girl should make her debut with full ceremony at the annual Debutantes' Ball at Government House, for upon the impression she created that night her whole future, it was felt, might well depend.

Ever since my sister Ruth's departure to England my parents had been looking forward to her returning, and my father had made a beautiful little mahogany writing-table and chair for her. Although I had been a closer companion to him, she and I shared his heart more than any of his other children, and he always liked to have us both beside him as much as possible.

My mother, too, was happy at the thought of Ruth's return, but her happiness had a more material basis; for she looked forward to the prospect of chaperoning Ruth to dances and of basking in the reflected glory of the admiration she aroused; and of contriving for her the best possible marriage. She loved her very dearly, but in her eyes marriage was the only object to be held in view where a daughter was concerned, and a 'good marriage' meant one that was socially and financially desirable. A daughter, too, was a potential *source féconde* who would provide her with grandchildren upon whom she could dote to her heart's content. She therefore kept a speculative eye upon all eligible bachelors and carefully contrasted their respective merits.

Ruth was now entrancingly pretty, and had lost none of that elusive quality which had distinguished her as a child. She had grown tall, but her figure, with its long flanks, small hips and bust, caused my mother some misgiving – for it did not accord with the fashions of the day; besides which Imp obstinately refused to wear the heavily boned, straight-fronted corsets which were then the correct thing.

A few weeks after her arrival I went with them to the *couturière* who had been chosen to make Imp's coming-out frock, and my mother confided her doubts to Madame. To her surprise and chagrin, Madame – who had arrived in the colony but a short time before to visit her French clientele there – took one long glance at Imp and declared that not only was she ravishing: but that her figure was that of a sylph, her type of beauty that of a Bacchante; and that she demanded clothes of an unique and distinctive design. Snatching up a pencil and paper she swiftly sketched a dress of long clinging lines and Grecian simplicity. Calling for soft silks and satins she draped them upon Imp and, standing back to observe the effect, expressed her delight in a flood of French.

But the last thing my mother was prepared to countenance was any deviation from the conventional. In dress, as in everything else, a daughter of hers must be *comme-il-faut*.

'Such a garment may be beautiful and becoming and might be successful in artistic circles in Paris or London,' she informed Madame coldly 'but it would be derided in Trinidad.'

In which I daresay she was right.

When the great day arrived all the old servants with their children and grandchildren gathered in our compound. All were dressed in their best and adorned with all their ornaments, and each had brought a gift. There were yams, sweet-potatoes, aubergines and beans from their plots of land: there were calabashes of eggs and even a few fowls: for such had always been the custom in the old days and the 'onward march of progress' had not yet rooted out personal loyalties or generous instincts.

Food and drink were provided for them, and the compound echoed with their talk and laughter. When Ruth went to greet them they milled round her with shining eyes and flashing teeth, presenting their gifts and exclaiming eagerly:

'E-e-h! I'se too glad to see yo'. I's come to wish yo' well' . . . 'I come all de ways from San Fernando to see yo' on yo' out-comin' . . . 'Darlin', dis be gran' day fo' we-all. If Gawd had only spared my fader to see it . . .'

Ruth tripped from one to another, her eyes alight with excitement, and my mother followed from time to time entreating:

'Ruth, *chérie*, you will wear yourself out before the night if you rush about so. Sit down on this chair and relax . . . put your feet up . . . have a cushion at your back . . . You must have a little glass of sherry and a biscuit . . . Nini will soon be here to dress you!' For this important task had been allotted to her, a younger woman.

At last, as the household was emerging from its afternoon siesta, Nini arrived in some state with her cousin Coralie and with 'Zabette's daughter, Mrs Clark. Completely composed, at once her personality dominated the scene. Tea was taken up to Ruth as she rested; then, after she had had a bath, Mrs Clark massaged her with eau-de-Cologne and she was ordered to relax once more, with pads soaked in rose-water over her eyes, until it was time for her to begin the actual dressing.

I had to submit to being washed and put into my nightgown at an unusually early hour, since Estelle's services were needed also; but determining to miss nothing of the proceedings, I ensconced myself in a corner of Ruth's bedroom and sat out of the way unremarked upon the floor.

A cheval mirror had been placed at right angles to the dressing-table, on which were tall candles. On a stand was a lamp with a reflector while two others had been set on nearby tables, so that all formed a circle of light about Ruth as, clad so far as her petticoat, she sat at the dressing-table. On one side of her stood Estelle waving a palm-leaf fan to keep her cool: on the other 'Truda similarly employed. Meanwhile Coralie, who had a flair for hairdressing, brushed Ruth's long ebony hair.

Upon the bed lay the dress, cloak, shoes and fan: and beside it, ready to play her part when called upon, waited Mrs Clark. My mother, already dressed in a gown of black silk with lacy décolletage and voluminous sleeves, was sitting for the sake of coolness in a doorway, where a sheet had been spread on the floor to protect her train from dust. As always when she was intent she looked a trifle grim, and her fingers gripped her lorgnettes firmly. Nini sat beside her, holding her head high with a defiant pride as though repudiating her deformity.

Coralie polished Ruth's hair with a silk handkerchief and arranged it high on her head in rolls. Several tendrils were then induced with the aid of curling tongs to lie on her forehead. These Ruth regarded with some misgiving, saying dubiously:

'If only I could be sure they would stay like that! What will happen to them when I get hot?'

'They *will* stay like that,' Coralie assured her. 'And you will *not* get hot. There is no *romping* at Government House, Ruth. They don't allow the Polka or the Barn Dance, and even the Lancers are danced very decorously.'

'It is *défendu* even to reverse in a waltz,' Nini put in, 'so set your mind at rest. Coralie, her hair looks perfect. You are an artist.' She got up and held a tiny wreath of roses, now here, now there, against Ruth's hair. 'Where are you going to have this? To the left side, I think, not too high up . . . yes! It's *chic* just there!'

Mrs Clark now came forward with the skirt of the dress over her hands, her dark finger-tips protruding beyond it; but Nini checked her momentarily with a gesture, saying, with a covert glance at my mother:

'Although some people might disapprove of it, I consider Ruth's arms and shoulders need whitening. When her frock is on they will look sallow by comparison. I have some French chalk here; so now, Estelle, fetch a little gin.'

Shocked and indignant, my mother intervened.

'Nini! How can you suggest such a thing! Do you want to give the impression that Ruth is . . . well . . . *fast*? A debutante's greatest charm is her look of fresh young innocence. There should be nothing artificial about her – *nothing*!'

'Don't be so ingenuous, Alice, and do be consistent. In the eighteenth century women made up lavishly, and in the twentieth they probably will again. It's nothing to do with innocence: it's purely a question of fashion. As for artificiality, Ruth has no bust to speak of, so frills have been stitched into her bodice to give the effect of one: God made her waist twenty-two inches, and we are going to lace it in until we have reduced it to eighteen!'

Without more ado she mixed the gin and the chalk into a smooth paste and proceeded to apply it with a tuft of cotton-wool, my mother maintaining a tight-lipped and disapproving silence. But when Nini poured some more gin into a saucer and dipped a piece of red ribbon into it she started to her feet with a cry of horror.

'Nini! This is too much! You can't be going to *rouge* the child?'

But Nini was already doing so, and Coralie interposed soothingly:

'Alice dear, a *soupçon* of colour will enhance Ruth's whole appearance! Remember, dear, she came back several months ago – she hasn't just returned from Europe with fine rosy cheeks, and vis-à-vis the debutantes who have she will look pale and washed out.'

The force of the argument quelled my mother's objections, but her face remained rigid with disapproval. For it was true: there would be girls whose parents months in advance had booked a mail-boat passage so that they would arrive just before the Ball, their looks as well-guarded a secret as the style of their frocks. When the ship arrived a concourse of young men would gather outside the Customs House to catch the first glimpse of these newly grown-up beauties as they disembarked, hurried ashore into hooded Victorias by their mothers, heads down, faces concealed by Leghorn hats – but wearing their prettiest ensembles!

Nini now signed to Mrs Clark to come forward with the skirt, which was carefully lowered over Ruth's head. As it was settled about her hips the two sides of the waistband were so far apart that it looked as though they could never be made to meet.

'Draw in your breath, Ruth,' Nini instructed, 'and *hold it*. The waistband will be torture until you are laced, but you must bear it.'

Ruth obeyed. Beads of sweat gathered on the faces of Coralie and Mrs Clark as they struggled to hook the skirt. Ruth gasped, then let out her breath with a rush.

'I can't hold it any longer! I feel as though my lungs were bursting!'

'You must, you *must*! Try again.'

'I'm getting so hot,' Ruth wailed. 'I'm starting to perspire! The chalk will congeal and I shall look awful! Estelle, you aren't fanning me properly!'

'Don't excite yourself so, Ruth,' Nini chided. 'Display a little fortitude. It's all being done for your benefit after all. Come now, try again.'

At last the struggle was crowned with success; and Mrs Clark was holding the bodice so that Ruth could put her arms into its puffed sleeves. It was stiffly boned, with eyelet holes running down both edges of the back where silk laces would be threaded. Nini and Coralie held the edges together while Mrs Clark threaded the laces criss-cross from top to bottom.

'Now then!' said Nini. 'Put your hands on your hips,' Ruth. I will count *one – two – three*. When I reach *three* draw in your breath *and hold it* while Mrs Clark pulls the laces tight. When I count again let your breath out *gradually*, have a moment's rest, then draw it in again and she will complete the tightening.'

She counted. Ruth gripped her waist with both hands. She pressed as she drew in her breath. Mrs Clark wound the laces round her hands and pulled steadily, and the gap between the two edges of the bodice began to close. A rest, then the process was continued, my mother meanwhile sitting on the edge of her chair, lips compressed, body rigid, lorgnettes to her eyes scrutinising everything. Coralie's hands were gripped together, her face strained. I was clasping my knees so tightly that I got pins and needles in my fingers. Estelle and 'Truda were gaping. The sweat was rolling down Mrs Clark's cheeks. Ruth was biting her lower lip. Nini alone appeared unperturbed and cool. At last 'Truda broke the silence with a nervous giggle.

'Eh-eh! Dis is a t'ing! How Miss Ruth gwine support all dat tightness!'

A final tug and the two sides of the bodice met, the laces were securely tied and on everyone's face the look of tension relaxed – except on Ruth's. But no-one noticed her symptoms of distress for all were exclaiming in admiration of her frock. It was, indeed, lovely. Of finest white silk muslin made in quantities of soft gathers over a foundation of stiff white glacé silk, the skirt, which flared widely to the ground, had row after row of tiny frills, each edged with narrow Valenciennes lace. The low cut bodice had a wide *berthe* composed of rows of the Valenciennes edging gathered on to pale pink net, embroidered here and there with minute sprays of rosebuds to match the wreath on Ruth's dark curls, and with tiny silver spangles which flashed splinters of light. Ruth's stockings were of transparent black silk, and her bronze slippers were ornamented with silver buckles set with brilliants which had once adorned a brocade waistcoat of her grandfather's. Cries of delight arose from everyone's lips.

'Perfect, my dear!' . . . 'What a line!' . . . 'How beautifully the skirt flares!' . . . 'It will be the loveliest dress at the Ball!' . . . 'Ruth your dress is a dream! You need fear no competition on that score at any rate!'

Nini brought the company back to earth.

'How goes the time?' she asked briskly. 'Another quarter of an hour . . . How do you feel, Ruth? You are getting used to it? *Bien!* Sit quietly a moment longer. I will titivate your face again, then you can show yourself to Lechmere . . . 'Zabette is waiting to see you in the dining-room. The others are all gathered on the front steps.' As she spoke, her fingers were busy putting the finishing touches to Ruth's face and hair. Mrs Clark was holding the point-lace fan and the long white kid gloves, and Coralie the cloak which matched the frock.

Ruth gasped:

'I don't know how I shall be able to *dance*! I can hardly *breathe*!'

'Come, come,' said Nini, 'do not look as though you were in

the hands of the Inquisition. Tight-lacing is something you must get used to. Think! Every eye will be upon you tonight!'

My mother said tenderly, giving Ruth's hand a little squeeze:

'Dear child, your frock couldn't be lovelier, and you look very, very sweet. Try to bear the discomfort.'

Ruth smiled. She kissed my mother's cheek.

'I'm getting more used to it,' she said, 'but oh! what a relief it will be when I can take it off and expand and expand!'

With my chin in my hand I gazed at Ruth – Ruth with her hair up! She was looking so bewitching that I loved her, and she was staring at her reflection in the mirror as though she did not recognise herself. Her dark eyes were shining, her lips were parted over her perfect teeth. Her little retroussé nose looked at once both childish and provocative. As Coralie placed the cloak about her shoulders she took a long last look at herself, her face alive with animation. Working her hands into her long gloves she went to show herself to my father and to 'Zabette. There were long-drawn breaths of admiration as she displayed herself to the gathering on the front steps before getting into the carriage with my mother. Then they drove off and the assembled concourse ran after them to the gate cheering and calling down benedictions – and suddenly Estelle had swooped down upon me and caught me up in her arms, crying:

'E-e-e-e! Miss Ruth look well sweet, but all-yo' wait till me girl here make she out-comin'! *Dat* will be a time!' And carrying me off she tucked me up in bed and gave me a sugar-cake to munch.

Suddenly I felt totally, utterly tired. What a day of concentrated attention!

Seating herself on the floor close by, Estelle began to sing in her warm, husky voice the *Wedding of the Humbug Bee.**

> *'De Humbug Bee humbug me'*
> *He say: 'Yo'll marry no one but me.'*
> *Um-hum, um-hum.*

---

* Humbug Bee – Bumble Bee. But 'to humbug' also means to annoy, as well as to deceive.

'An 'where shall de weddin' party be?'
Um-hum, um-hum.
'Down dere underneat' de coconut tree.'
Um-hum, um-hum.
'An' who shall de weddin' party be?'
Um-hum, um-hum.

De firs' dat come was Mistah Ant,
He look so nice in he bran' new Pant'
Um-hum, um-hum.
De nex' dat come was Mistah Flea,
He play he fiddle across he knee.
Um-hum, um-hum.
De nex' dat come was Mosquito-Man,
He lick up de gravy from de fryin'-pan.
Um-hum, um-hum.
De las' dat come was Mistah Bug,
He drink-up de rum in' de 'mash-up jug.
Um-hum, um-hum.

So Estelle sang, and while the familiar words and rhythm of the old negro tune passed through my head I pictured Ruth dancing in her white frock, her eyes shining . . . In a few years time – oh! a long, long time afterwards! – it would be my turn. . . . And so I fell asleep.

CHAPTER SEVENTEEN

Land of my Fathers

From the moment of her début Ruth was besieged by admirers. The four men from the Chummery were, as my mother phrased it, 'at her feet'. But the best *parti* in my mother's eyes was Paddy. He had private means, he came of a good family and his career was promising. That he was seventeen years older than Ruth constituted no drawback in her eyes. Had she not herself married a man seventeen years her senior? Could any marriage have been more successful? Marriage, children and a home were the very foundations of life in her view. The fact that she was of a different generation and of a totally different temperament from Ruth did not occur to her.

My father had the greatest liking for Paddy and had not the slightest doubt that he would make a most tender and devoted husband. But he had a far deeper insight into Ruth's character. He realised how immature she still was, and how complex – perhaps incapable yet of true loving. For him marriage, children and a home were just as desirable, but they arose in a natural sequence out of a man and a woman's love for each other – not vice versa.

In Ruth he discerned much of his own mother's restless and impetuous disposition. There had been no urgent reason to dwell on this before, but he did now, and deeply. He felt that Ruth needed time, that she was incomplete, that in her some seed was awaiting development of which she herself was unaware, but before this had happened she could never really be herself. Looking back I see this potential as in her dancing. But I doubt if he did, for a career in dancing in those days was even less respectable than one in acting.

Ruth's formative years of adolescence, unfortunately, had been in England, beyond his observation and influence, and not even at a boarding school, where her talents and interests might have been discovered, but in the home of two elderly spinsters in Shropshire. From that disciplined and repressive existence she had now stepped straight into the limelight as one of the loveliest girls of her year. Excited by the flattery and attentions of admirers on the one hand, and with her every whim gratified by a doting mother on the other, it is not surprising that she was swept out of her depth. Nor is it surprising that, with my mother's skilful suggestions working continually on her mind, she should have accepted Paddy – in the firm belief that marriage with him would provide her with all that she needed in life.

'Are you *certain* that this marriage is really for Ruth's happiness?' my father would ask.

'Naturally,' my mother confidently replied on each occasion. 'If Ruth hunted the world through she couldn't find a more charming man than Paddy. Every other girl has been setting her cap at him! We must not put our own wishes first.'

'That's all begging the question. I'm thinking of her *happiness* in the long run.' he would say, trying to make her understand his doubts.

'Stop it, Lechmere. Surely he is the one man most qualified to make her happy? He's utterly in love with her. His disposition is sympathetic. He is gentle and generous. He will be patient and tender with her. What *more* could one ever hope for?'

'I was thinking of her happiness in a more positive sense.'

'What is positive happiness? Ruth is too much like your mother ever to be positively happy. No-one can expect to have everything exactly as they would like it! Under the influence of Paddy's love, and with the birth of a child, she will develop into a very contented woman. Love will come, you'll see.'

My father sighed. It was impossible to argue with my mother on such a subject as this, for there was no common ground. He was helpless. Besides, my mother might very well be right. He could only sit back and let events take their course.

Six months later the marriage took place, and Ruth and Paddy went to live in an old plantation house, dating from the time when the Savannah had been a sugar estate, that stood on a part of the later site of the Queen's Park Hotel.

Visiting them there I saw 'Romance' in real life for the first time – for Ruth was on a pedestal. It was a halcyon age for women at the turn of the century between the formality of earlier restrictiveness and the total disappearance of the barriers between the sexes; and certainly it influenced my early ideas on marriage!

Soon after the marriage my father fell ill, and was laid up for several weeks. His strength gave out, and he developed a long debilitating fever. Lying in bed he continued to grieve, despite his great liking for Paddy. He began to think back to his childhood in England when he had beheld his mother on her successive visits from Trinidad becoming more moody, more frustrated – until the taste for life had become so bitter in her mouth that death had been a release. He feared that something similar might happen with Ruth.

Ruth's presence had diffused an aura of enchantment in the house, and had distracted him from other inner worries, and the very complexity of her character had provided a varied stimulation: her sudden gaiety, her moments of intimacy or touches of melancholy, the melting glance of her eyes, the grace of her movements, were alike irresistible. Just as when bright sunshine illuminates a room, flashing back its radiance from ornaments, gleaming on polished furniture, and then a cloud suddenly plunges the whole into shadow, so it was when she left us. The house became suddenly still.

It was nine years since my father's resignation and somehow the bitterness of the controversy surrounding that event had never quite dissipated. He had built up and fought for a secular system of education, and suddenly he had been overridden, and control of many schools put into the hands of clergy, particularly Roman Catholic clergy, who he feared would not respect intellectual freedom as he did. And he had been proved right.

Although accepting his job had enabled him to marry, he would never have contemplated doing so had he not been

Piedmont Cottage, with a gardener and a marchande

A typical 'down-the-islands' house on Monos

Martinique dress worn by
cousin Theodora Walter

Ruth's Ball Card, 1897.
The other dates are: 1498
Columbus discovering the
island; 1797 capture of the
island by the British

At Ruth and Paddy's wedding on June 21, 1898:
in the back row on the left are Theodora Walter and Gareth Guppy;
seated next to bridegroom Alice Guppy;
on the right Lucy Walter, Theodora's mother;
Yseult in front of the bride

Glenside Lodge, entrance drive

An oyster marchand
counting change

Beebee, the Hindu girl

convinced of its intrinsic, and permanent worth. It had ruined his prospects of an academic career in science. Not that he regretted it, for it had given him Alice, so mature for her age, so womanly, so full of common sense – whereas Ruth . . .

He was, without question, highly unsettled. It was a crisis in which he reviewed his life, his hopes, all around him. He toyed with the idea of studying law, and taking up his father's abandoned practice. My mother was at her wits' end. So when at last he began to get up again, she decided that a trip to England would help him convalesce and forget all these brooding doubts.

I had been there once before, and although I was only four when he had left I retained some vivid recollections of that visit. We had rented a house in West Kensington, with a small garden and a copper beech under which I played, to be near the home of my father's aunt, Maria Gibbon. She came nearly every day to see us, the most lovable and entertaining old lady imaginable, who lived to be over a hundred.

She was small with acquiline features, exquisite manners and a lively sense of humour. She did intricate and delicate needlework, and presented me with a set of small dolls dressed in the fashion of a mid-nineteenth century household. They consisted of parents, children and a complete domestic staff including a page-boy in buttons, and details of their dresses were correct down to the minutest particular.

Aunt Maria possessed an encyclopaedic knowledge of the Royal Family, and she always tried to be present when 'our dear Queen' made one of her rare public appearances. She took me with her on one such occasion – I have forgotten what – and I went eagerly, never doubting that the Great Queen would be wearing a little crown above a white lace veil, and the blue ribbon of the Garter across her bodice, as she appeared in every coloured print. I was therefore immeasurably disappointed to find her in a black cape and bonnet almost exactly like those of Aunt Maria herself, and that she was just as small. Nevertheless she contrived to convey an air of majesty which compelled the attention even more than the splendour of her Indian orderlies.

I remembered how my brother Gareth, returning from the Egyptian Hall where Maskelyne and Cook were at the height of their fame, described how he had seen a conjurer put a sixpence up his nose and extract half-a-crown from his ear. I had no sixpence, but resolved to see what would materialise if I did the same with a boot-button. Not without some pain I pushed one as far as I could up my nose and, with a finger-tip in each ear awaited results expectantly. But the only thing that happened was that the pain in my nose increased and I grew frightened, and because of my fright told no-one what I had done. When my nurse was bathing me at bedtime, the pain, as she washed my face, caused me to scream to such a purpose, that although I still remained obstinately silent, a doctor was sent for, when awed either by himself or his office, I confessed, and the button was extracted, disappointingly unchanged.

When straw had been spread in the street before a house near ours, and I was told that it was because the lady who lived there had had a baby, I had marvelled that such a prodigious quantity of straw was needed to pack a baby in; and at the same time shocked at the idea of it being just tumbled out of doors and allowed to lie in the street.

Many other scenes also lingered in my mind: the grim, starved faces of the men in tattered garments who ran behind our 'growler' (cab) for miles in the hope of earning a copper or two by carrying the luggage indoors; street-Arabs turning cartwheels along the pavements for pennies, and barefooted children with wan, pinched faces staring hungrily and with unchildlike eyes into the pastrycooks' windows, crowded with cakes and confectionery, while the fragrance of baking rose richly through the gratings underneath. German bands played brassily at street corners. On hot days horses wore hats, on wet days loin cloths; and at all seasons ate continually out of nosebags which they tossed from time to time – an immediate signal for a flock of sparrows and pigeons to swoop down and hunt among the chaff for an occasional spilt oat. Lamplighters emerged out of winter fogs and deftly flicked on the street lamps with their long poles, leaving in their train golden globes of light, each shrouded in a misty nimbus.

There stood out sharply that miracle of beauty, the wonder of which enchants me still: frost-patterns on the window-panes. And I can still recall my astounded bewilderment when I awoke for the first time to a world of snow – to the silent, persistent fall of flakes and the eerie unnatural light which illuminated the white world and the yellowy sky above.

On the day of our departure, the 20th April, I celebrated my ninth birthday. 'The *Don* and *Magdalena*, great steamers white and gold,' wrote Rudyard Kipling; and it was by the *Don* that we sailed.

The Royal Mail Steam Packet Company, which owned these vessels, proudly held a Royal Charter and considered itself almost on a par with the Royal Navy. Life on board its ships was conducted with some ceremony, which resulted in the female passengers finding a change of frock at least three times a day an unavoidable necessity. So in the mornings they appeared on deck in smart hats with gloves and parasols, as though they were going for a stroll in Hyde Park; changed into something fluffier for tea; and, of course, into full evening dress for dinner. Church Parade on Sundays, when the entire ship's company lined up on deck for inspection by the captain, was as impressive a spectacle as it could well be. The uniform of the officers was nearly identical with that worn by the Navy on such ceremonial occasions: frock-coats and swords, white covers on their caps and white gloves on their hands. Only their cap-badges and the gold braid denoting their ranks were different. Inspection over, all trooped to the dining-saloon where Divine Service was conducted by the captain.

The voyage over, Southampton, where we docked, was a breathlessly exciting scene of ships large and small; of whistles blowing and people hurrying; of imperturbable policemen and bustling railway porters, conspicuous in green waistcoats and scarlet ties.

How fast, luxurious and smooth-running was the train which rushed us to London! How long it was, and how huge its engine! What numbers of other trains flashed by with shattering percussions! What hundreds of shining rails curving into what acres of sidings; what thousands of houses crowded together, and how queer those little things on top called chimney-pots! But more wonderful still were the green fields with their embroidery of daisies and buttercups, bordered with hedges where tall trees stood sentinel and May blossom frothed pink and white. I longed to adopt as a pet one of those frisking lambs, and was awed by the massive size of the cart-horses, huge enough to belong to a world of giants. I thought no-one in the world looked so happy as the children, with glowing rosy cheeks, balancing on gates and waving to us as we raced past.

As I kneeled on the carriage seat gazing out of the window a strange feeling came over me: I *knew* that this was my country: I *knew* that however much I loved Trinidad here only could my home ultimately be; that wherever fate might take me in the days to come, the roots of my being were deeply implanted here – and would eventually pull me back.

> *I am the land of their fathers,*
> *In me the virtue stays;*
> *I will bring back my children*
> *After certain days.*

My father's time was fully occupied. He was entertained by many of his scientific friends; he read papers before various societies, and spent many hours at the South Kensington Natural History and Geological Museums where some of his specimens were displayed. Yet in spite of all this he found time to take me to the Zoo – exercising a member's privilege by going on Sundays – and to show me other of the sights of London. On one of these occasions an adventure befell us.

He had obtained a permit for us to be taken over certain parts of the Tower of London which were not open to the general public. When we had nearly completed our tour the Beefeater who had been detailed to escort us met another, in charge of a similar party who were just beginning theirs, and handed over to him the huge key of the outer door. Our Beefeater was deeply versed in the history and legends of the Tower, and when my father happened to mention that Sir Thomas Overbury, (who had been slowly poisoned to death there in King James I's reign) had been an ancestor of ours, this led to so prolonged an excursion into historical backwaters, and this in turn to our retracing our steps to behold something overlooked on our first tour, that when we finally reached the heavy oaken door leading to the outer world we found it locked against us.

Our guide was much perturbed, and told us that he feared our plight would not be discovered until many hours later, when the next roll-call disclosed that he himself was missing. Meanwhile we were prisoners: prisoners in the Tower of London; in its very deepest dungeons! Today what other child – or grown-up, for that matter, – could boast such an experience?

As there was nothing else to be done we seated ourselves on an ancient chest and took up the conversation where we had left it. But now I noticed for the first time how hollowly our voices echoed in that dank place; and when they paused, how empty and ominous the silence seemed to be. The twilit gloom seemed to deepen about us, and it was hard to believe that the world outside was filled with summer sunshine. Dark shadows, unnoticed before, took on threatening shapes, drawing nearer as though to ensnare us and crush us beneath the weight of human misery of which these stones had been the witnesses down so many centuries. All that I had heard and read of this place was in an instant changed: the romantic, fairy-tale quality of the Tower of London vanished, and in its place appeared something stark and terrible – a tale of pain, suffering and conflict unendingly endured. I sought and clutched my father's hand tightly, and when at long last the grating of the key in the ponderous lock of the outer door heralded our release, history had acquired for me a new significance.

This visit provided me with my first opportunity to see something of the English countryside: to roam in those fields and to gather those flowers which hitherto I had glimpsed only from my seat in the railway carriage; to stand beneath tall trees and to know with my finger-tips the different quality of each one's bark – the green smoothness of beech, the furrowed male roughness of oak or elm, the mottled slenderness of silver birch. Now for the first time I knew the smell of England in June: the scent of hayfields, of meadow-sweet, of growing corn and dusty fallows; of newly mown lawns and great beds of flowers. Now for the first time I saw the wild rose.

This is how it happened: my grandfather had had two older brothers, both of whom had died before my birth, but whose children we sometimes saw. The middle one, Thomas Richard Guppy, was a distinguished engineer in the middle years of the 19th century. In 1830 he had founded the Great Western Railway, organising the first meetings in Bristol and putting up £14,300 to cover the first costs of formation. In 1835, even more ambitious, he and his partner Isambard Kingdom Brunel had founded the Great Western Steamship Company, and began building the first great transatlantic steamships, the *Great Western* (1837), and the *Great Britain* (1843), which has been described as the first modern ship. A modest man, plagued with ill health, he has been over-shadowed by his highly flamboyant associate, but indeed not only did he actually build the *Great Britain* but many of its most advanced design features were his ideas or inventions – the water tight compartments, the use of a propeller instead of paddle wheels, and much else. Finally in 1849, after help-ing Brunel build his unsuccessful Atmospheric Railway in Devon, my great-uncle's consumption became so bad that he was forced to leave England. He retired to a villa outside Naples, and founded a large ship building and engineering firm there which built naval vessels, the Florence Market, and much else.

Samuel Guppy Jnr, my grandfather's eldest brother, also started life as an engineer, but then his career took an entirely different direction, for his first wife, Georgina Protheroe, was strongly psychic. A rich man, he retired at the age of forty-five, and thenceforward devoted himself to investigating the mysteries of spirit drawings, seances, etc. He was a highly sceptical man, and he endeavoured to explain such events rationally – indeed materialistically – and he expressed these doubts and explanations in one of the earliest books on Spiritualism – *Mary Jane, or Spiritualism Chemically Explained* (1863).

His doubts however were completely quelled when he met the remarkable medium Agnes Nichol, who eventually became his second wife. A great deal has been written about her, some of it vituperative, because vituperation ran high in the highly competitive and sometimes lucrative business of being a medium in Victorian times. However in the event she was the only great Victorian medium who was never exposed in any fraudulent practice. Perhaps the most telling description of her is that of Alfred Russel Wallace, the co-founder with Charles Darwin of the Theory of Evolution by means of Natural Selection. In *Miracles and Modern Spiritualism* (1901) he wrote:

The last medium to whose career I shall call attention is Mrs Guppy (formerly Miss Nichol), and in this case I can give some personal testimony. I knew Miss Nichol before she had ever heard of spiritualism, table-rapping, or anything of the kind, and we first discovered her powers on asking her to sit for experiment in my house. This was in November 1866, and for some months we had constant sittings, and I was able to watch and test the progress of her development. I first satisfied myself of the rising of a small table completely off the floor when three or four persons (including Miss N.) placed their hands on it. I tested this by secretly attaching threads or thin strips of paper beneath the claws, so that they must be broken if any one attempted to raise the table with their feet – the only available means of doing so. The table still rose a full foot off the floor in broad daylight. In order to show this to friends with less trouble, I made a cylinder of hoops and brown paper, in which I placed the table so as to keep feet and dresses away from it while it rose, which it did as freely as before . . .

The most remarkable feature of this lady's mediumship was the production of flowers and fruits in closed rooms. The first time this occurred was at my own house, at a very early stage of her development. All present were my own friends. Miss N. had come early to tea, it being mid-winter, and she had been with us in a very warm gas-lighted room four hours before the flowers appeared. The essential fact is, that upon a bare table in a small room closed and dark (the adjoining room and passage being well lighted), a quantity of flowers appeared, which were not there when we put out the gas a few minutes before. They consisted of anemones, tulips, chrysanthemums, Chinese primroses, and several ferns. All were absolutely fresh, as if just gathered from a conservatory. They were covered with a fine cold dew. Not a petal was crumpled or broken, not the most delicate point or pinnule of the ferns was out of place. I dried and preserved the whole, and have attached to them the attestation of all present that they had no share, as far as they knew, in bringing the flowers into the room. I believed at the time, and still believe that it was absolutely impossible for Miss N. to have concealed them so long, to have kept them so perfect, and, above all, to produce them covered throughout with a most beautiful coating of dew, just like that which collects on the outside of a tumbler when filled with very cold water on a hot day.

Similar phenomena have occurred hundreds of times since, in many houses and under various conditions. Sometimes the flowers have been in vast quantities, heaped upon the table. Often flowers or fruits asked for are brought. A friend of mine asked for a sunflower, and one six feet high fell upon the table, having a large mass of earth about its roots. One of the most striking tests was at Florence, with Mr T. Adolphus Trollope, Mrs Trollope, Miss Blagden, and Colonel Harvey. The room was searched by the gentlemen; Mrs Guppy was undressed and redressed by Mrs Trollope, every article of her clothing being examined. Mr and Mrs Guppy were both firmly held while at the table. In about ten minutes all the party exclaimed that they smelt flowers, and, on lighting a candle, both Mrs Guppy's and Mr Trollope's arms were found covered with jonquils, which filled the rooms with their odour.

Although I never witnessed any such happening, I found Elizabeth, as her family knew her, a most warm and kindly person. By my great-uncle she had had two sons, Tom and Sam, who were only three and five when he died. It is of Sam whom I now speak, for my parents were very fond of him, and we always saw him when in England.

At the age of twenty-five he married Septima Robinson, a woman of considerable fortune and some years older than himself. Sam was an unassuming and pleasant person, tall and strong, and only happy out-of-doors. He farmed his wife's land. Farmers can be as inspired as artists, though they are usually less articulate. For Sam, the land and all connected with it had as great a creative stimulus as paper and pen to a writer, or canvas and paint to a painter. The freshly turned furrows, stretching in long, straight lines from hedgerow to hedgerow were to him as beautiful a work of art as the Venus of Milo; as gratifying as doubtless the Venus had been to the sculptor whose hands and brain had wrought her.

Mrs Sam was in her natural element on the back of a horse. She hunted regularly with the local pack, and it was owing to a hunting accident that she had lost her hope of having a child. She looked impressive on horseback. Towards Sam she tended to be domineering and possessive, and her general disposition was distinctly contentious. She and Sam lived in a delightful Georgian house a few miles from Malden, in Surrey – in those days a quiet country town set in a quiet countryside – and with them, occupying a suite of her own, lived Mrs Sam's elder sister, who was a chronic invalid. She spent most of her time on a chaise-longue, reading and writing, but on fine days drove out in a little pony carriage drawn by a pair of Shetlands. Often she took me with her, and sometimes we drove into Malden where the tradesmen came out of the shops to wait attentively upon her at the carriage's side. Or sometimes we visited cottages in the neighbourhood, taking gifts to the children of little frocks that she had sewn herself.

I stayed there several times during that summer. Then unexpectedly shortly before our return to Trinidad, Mrs Sam came to London to see my father and mother, and announced to their astonishment that she wished to adopt me. She would make a settlement upon me then and there, and I should inherit the remainder of her estate upon her death. She was clearly well-intentioned and very serious, and my mother was pleased and flattered that I should be so much liked and wanted. Time was asked for, so as not to dismiss the offer too abruptly but it was eventually declined. My own feelings in the matter were not consulted. Privately I was alarmed. I should have enjoyed the beautiful house, the gardens, the farms – but not at the expense of giving up my parents. Besides at the best of times Mrs Sam rather frightened me!

So my chance of becoming a rich young woman vanished, and Mrs Sam was so indignant at our refusal that she severed all connections with us forthwith, and made her husband do the same.

A year or two later Sam wrote to us from Canada. He had parted from his wife and his whole letter breathed the spirit of release. As for Mrs Sam – she for her part adopted three children from an orphanage, sublimated her energies into the cause of anti-vivisection, and eventually left her fortune to other relations and to numerous causes connected with her good works.

Our return voyage was without incident until our ship was entering the Bocas. Then all the passengers were summoned to the saloon and informed that, owing to a death from yellow fever in the third class, we were all to be landed on the Five Islands and placed in quarantine.

The grown-ups were thrown into a state of indignation and alarm: indignation because the eagerly awaited climax of the voyage was now ruined, long cherished plans must be abandoned, and all the preparations made to welcome them by family and friends ashore, who were even now awakening in a state of happy anticipation, were to be brought to naught; alarm because yellow fever was a deadly scourge, dreaded throughout the tropics, claiming its victims swiftly and nearly always fatally. But to us children yellow fever meant little, while a holiday 'down the islands' was a familiar and unqualified delight, and we were consequently overjoyed at so dramatic and unexpected a piece of good fortune which would maroon us 'down the islands' for three whole glorious weeks!

The ship hove to, and we were landed on the islands from her boats, with victuals, bedding and hand luggage; then we watched her steam away to her anchorage.

Each day the medical officer came by launch to examine us and take our temperatures. He was a young and cheerful man with a tactful disposition which soothed ruffled tempers and made him popular with all. One day my mother said to him:

'They ought to send an older man than you to attend us. A young life like yours should not be risked.'

He laughed and declared that the risk was so negligible as to be practically non-existent; yet he, and he only, contracted the fever and died.

CHAPTER EIGHTEEN

Country Living

———◦◦◦◦———

During our absence abroad my aunt Marie had married a young American, Harry Lee, of the family of Robert E. Lee, the Confederate Commander, and gone with him to New York where Nini had joined them. Their subsequent story has no place in these pages, and it is enough to say that for the remainder of their lives these three were never separated, that they founded and ran two highly successful hotels, the Hotels Dysart, in Paris and London, and that none of them ever returned to Trinidad.

While in England my father had occupied himself, as usual, with his scientific interests, but on his return to Trinidad it was evident that his mind, hitherto always fixed so thoroughly on what he was doing, was lacking its customary concentration. Before long we learned the reason, for he electrified the household with the announcement that he had decided to buy a cocoa plantation and that we should go and live upon it.

My mother was appalled. Not only did she have no inclination whatever to be uprooted from Port-of-Spain and out of a mode of life which she found completely agreeable and to which she had been long accustomed, but she instantly foresaw a repetition of the disaster which had attended my grandparents' excursion into estate ownership, and her lively imagination conjured up visions of wholesale ruin like her father's, and of living her last years, as she put it, in 'some shack in a back street'. But for once all her arguments, pleadings and lamentations failed to shake my father's resolve. The most he would concede was that the place he chose should be within reasonable distance of Port-of-Spain and on the railway.

After inspecting a number of properties he finally purchased one named, somewhat unimaginatively, Glenside, near the small town of Tunapuna which was on the railway and only about fifteen miles south of Port-of-Spain. His first act as a landed proprietor did nothing to allay my mother's misgivings. Intending to build a new house for our occupation and wishing to enclose an acre or so of the land he had chosen for its site, almost before the ink was dry on the Deeds he sent to England for a tall iron fence. Flinging up her hands in horror my mother cried aloud to high Heaven:

'*Mon Dieu Seigneur!* History repeats itself! This is the beginning of the end!'

There was a tiny thatched cottage at the entrance to the estate which my father called the Lodge, and thither he frequently went for a night or two while the main house was being built. My mother manifested her disapproval by refusing to accompany him, and, indeed, by assuming an air of martyrdom whenever he went. But she found this attitude very difficult to sustain, for not only was she nervous and anxious all the time he was away, picturing him the victim of every description of unlikely accident, but in spite of herself she was gradually infected with his own enthusiasm – after all she came of a family of planters – and her opposition collapsed completely when Jim and Gareth suggested that they should occupy the Lodge and travel to and from Port-of-Spain every day, while friends offered eager congratulations upon the venture:

'My dear Alice, we hear Lechmere has bought a place in the country, and is making a lovely bathing pool in the river, and that there are glorious views! What wonderful parties you will be able to give there! Much more enjoyable than down the islands, for there won't be that hot and tedious trip by the *Ant*!'

Soon my mother had made a complete *volte-face* and was throwing herself so eagerly into the project that the tables were completely turned, and before long it was my father who began to wear a look of dismay and to utter reminders that he was not made of money.

'Lechmere, you must take me to see the place . . . It is essential that I should supervise the laying out of the garden. The roses must be *massed*. A long bed devoted entirely to *Caroline Testout*! Another to *La France*! . . . *Frau Karl Drushki* requires to be grouped in circular beds – so does *Gloire de Dijon* . . . *Maréchal Niel* must be grown over arches mingled with honeysuckle . . .'

She would pause, picturing the effect, then her mind would make a lightning dart in another direction:

'And the question of furniture! We need new loose covers . . . we must write for patterns of Cretonnes: they are more suitable for the country than Chintz – and we must order more linen. With people constantly to stay we must have more sheets, more pillowcases and towels . . .'

At all times of day a brisk tapping of high heels would announce her descent upon the study with a new idea, while at any hour of the night she might suddenly shake my father into wakefulness and proclaim:

'Lechmere! I've had an inspiration! We must . . .!'

Her next step was to decide the destinies of the servants. The entire Laycock family – except, of course, Jimmy, the philanderer – was to be uprooted and transferred to a cottage on the estate where Laycock would become estate carpenter with Ernest as his assistant; Mrs Laycock – meekly acquiescing amid fusillades of finger-cracking – would become our laundress aided by her eldest daughter, Maude; Edith, the second girl, would do the mending and make herself generally useful. Ella would become housemaid, and Alice – the youngest of the family and named after my mother – would dance attendance upon me in place of Estelle who was to be handed over to Ruth. Cook of course would go with us, and indeed she declared she would 'feel naked' if she did not; and so would Lavinia, whom alone my father would permit to sweep and dust his study, and who was confident that no-one else but she was fit 'to look after de master'. Augustus Bellborder had to remain behind because he was caretaker of the Boys' Model School – one of the institutions founded by my father – and since he had 'lost his drawin'-room floor' and, with it all interest in polishing, he took the parting philosophically.

Ruth was to take over the disbursement of the pensions – but our departure was a sad day for the pensioners. Deeply did they deplore our going; sorely would they miss us and their hours on the back verandah, though comforted by my mother's assurance that there would always be a room available for them in our new home where they could come and 'spend time'.

I was overjoyed at the prospect of living in the country, and indeed the happiest years of my life were spent at Glenside. I first saw the place with my father while he was still deliberating whether to buy it or not, and later he took me with him to stay at the Lodge while work progressed in the main house – which consisted, in the family tradition, of two houses connected by a covered way, the larger containing the living quarters, and the smaller my father's study and some extra guest-rooms. There were, of course, the usual deep, shady verandahs on which life in the West Indies is for the most part lived.

To the east the house looked out towards a distant range of mountains. To the north it commanded a view of the plantation itself: low hills, verdant and tranquil, their slopes planted with cocoa, and cleft by a valley at the bottom of which meandered a stream. My bedroom faced east and had a door into that of my parents, and as soon as they were in residence at the first hint of dawn I was through it and into their bed demanding 'coffee-sugar!'

At sunrise our *petit-déjeuner* was ready on the verandah; then my father pulled on his high boots and buckled his leather belt, with his cutlass and pruning knife in their respective sheaths. I, to my pride, wore a somewhat similar belt with a sheath to take my miniature cutlass. Thus equipped we set out on our round of the estate. Under the misty shade of the cocoa trees, which the rising sun was piercing with quivering golden spears, the air was moist and cool. Our feet fell soundlessly on the thick carpet of leaves through which ferns were thrusting their fronds and where the cocoa-lilies, with petals like long satin streamers, were drenching the air with their heady perfume. At this hour all was fresh and tender. I walked with light, dancing steps, life glowing within me as though showers of sparks raced through my veins, my mind alert, my glance everywhere.

Squirrels with big round eyes peeped at us from behind tree trunks, then scampered into the branches where they sat flicking their tails and scolding harshly; insects hummed and shrilled; birds chirped and fluttered as they took the first grateful warmth of the sun on the outflung branches of the immortelle trees which arched high overhead to give shade to the cocoa; *ramier* pigeons repeated endlessly:

> *Chookety Coo! Chookety Coo!*
> *Pigeon fly without a wing!*

Sometimes *lapp**, the local rabbit, lolloped across our path, sometimes *quenk***, the little wild pig, blundered through the undergrowth and, more rarely, a deer with huge alert ears and large frightened eyes would prance away on slender legs. Huge butterflies – the Emperor (*Morpho*), a brilliant blue; the Mortbleu (*Caligo*), purple and sapphire – fluttered with slow wing-beats in seemingly aimless indolence. Cocoa pods in all stages of ripeness, and ranging in colour from deep green to maroon and gold, hung from trunks and branches. Sometimes loud, sometimes muted, came the perpetual murmur of the stream as it wound its way, now babbling gaily over beds of white pebbles, now whispering softly over stretches of sand.

Never could there have been a happier blending of duty and pleasure than these morning excursions which were leading us to whatever part of the plantation was being 'worked' that day. Pruning might be going on, or thinning the young pods; or a gang of labourers might be 'brushing', which is cutlassing the undergrowth. Harvesting, too, was usually in progress, for besides the two main annual crops there were several small pickings. Negroes, equipped with cutlasses and *goulettes*, blades on long poles, severed the stout stems of the pods while others gathered them up, deftly sliced them open and tossed them on to a heap around which squatted women who scooped out the slimy beans and threw

* Paca
** Peccary

them into panniers woven from lianes, casting aside the empty pods to form brightly coloured pyramids. When the panniers were full they were slung across the backs of donkeys which were waiting in a patient, drowsy line, swishing their tails, and so taken to the sweating boxes, where the beans were kept before being freed from slime.

I loved to have a hand in all these operations. I might lead a laden donkey up the long hill and ride him back for the next load; I might reap the pods within my reach and slice them open, which I learned to do quite as adroitly as the labourers themselves. I could read the thermometer in the sweating boxes and loved to report the temperature to my father before Morgan, the overseer, did so. And when the beans were ready for drying I would join the men 'dancing the cocoa'. Morgan would strum a calypso on his *quatro*, and the labourers would tread the beans spread out on the drying-floor in time with his playing, writhing their bodies to the tune as the movement of their dancing feet rubbed away the slimy film. They sang in throaty voices, cracked jokes and guffawed with laughter. Then the beans were raked to turn them over so that they should dry evenly on both sides, and Morgan strummed even more energetically lest the sound of his *quatro* be drowned by the rattling of the beans. But all the time he kept a wary eye upon the hills, for there the showers gathered before sweeping down upon the valleys. Whenever one seemed to threaten he gave a warning shout, and the men would drop their rakes and run to either end of the drying-floor to pull together the two halves of the sliding roof which ran outwards and inwards on rails, for the least moisture would mildew the beans.

In a good sample of cocoa each bean is clean and mahogany-coloured, the *testa* crisp and brittle so that at a sharp pinch it will come away from the 'flesh', which should be a typical chocolate colour and firm, yet easy to break between the fingers of one hand. Trinidad cocoa is famous for its quality, and there used to be much friendly rivalry between the planters as to who could produce the best sample. Twice a day my father tested the cocoa on the drying-floor himself, and when he gave the word the bagging began. When this was completed my father would take samples up to Port-of-

Spain and bargain with the various exporters.

It was usual in those days for an estate to increase its acreage under cultivation by a method known as the Contract System. Under this the owner would hire out the parcel of land to be cultivated to the contractor at a nominal rent – say a couple of shillings a year – and the contractor would clear it, till it and plant it with cocoa seedlings provided by the owner. To give each seedling the shade it needed he would plant beside it a banana or plantain stool, and between these he would grow his annual crops. The yield of all these would be his. At the end of five years, by which time the young cocoa trees would be coming into bearing, he would receive – or did in those days – five dollars for each live tree and the contract would cease.

There were a number of such tenants on the estate. These were all East Indians, and they lived in neat little white-washed houses built of mud and thatch, and set amidst the plots of land from which they earned their livelihood by growing maize, pigeon peas, aubergines and other vege-tables. Some of them kept a cow, or even two, and all had goats and fowls. They were orderly, civil and hardworking. They did not pilfer from the estate, which was the invariable practice of the negroes: and they possessed dignity and grace; the young men were usually handsome and the girls exceed-ingly pretty.

My mother took a great interest in them, and before the birth of each new baby she set Edith Laycock to work making the quaint little gaily-coloured shirts which were their tradi-tional garments, while the inevitable packets of brown sugar were distributed among the expectant mothers. At Christmas time she invited them all to a party which was held beneath the cocoa house and there – religious differences being ignored on both sides – she distributed presents from a gaily decorated Christmas tree.

Among them was an old couple who had suffered the melancholy fate of outliving all their children, save for a single grandchild, a girl named Beebee, twelve years old, of singular beauty and with the grace and elegance of a fawn. One day the old couple came to announce that a marriage was to take place between Beebee and a youth from Orange Grove Estate in the neighbouring township. We knew of course that the East Indians matured and married at a very early age; nevertheless Beebee seemed as much a child as myself and it was a shock to think of her being married. Her grandparents asked to be allowed to build a hut near their own for Beebee and her bridegroom. He would cultivate the land and their savings would provide a cow as a marriage portion.

There was a fairy-tale quality about the whole proceedings which fascinated me. They were Hindus, and according to custom Beebee and her bridegroom – who was sixteen – would see each other for the first time only when he was brought to their new home after the conclusion of their separate marriage ceremonies. Those at the bridegroom's home lasted a week or more, and we were invited to attend on the final evening. It was a lovely, still, starlit night, and a great concourse of East Indians was gathered in a circle around an open space of hard-beaten earth. In the centre of this sat the youth, his feet tucked beneath him, surrounded by a ring of flickering lights which glinted upon his oil-polished skin. His body was clad only in a loin-cloth, but upon his head was a high tinsel crown sewn with pink frangipani blossoms, which hung in a fringe to his shoulders. He sat as motionless as a statue, with lowered eyes, his face stamped with a calmness as ineffable as that of Buddha himself.

The beating of drums, the babble of talk, ebbed and flowed about him; priests came and went, murmuring chants; brass platters piled high with rice, sacrificial meats and little cakes were set before him; dancers with bells on their ankles and flowers in their hair whirled around him until their skirts stood out stiffly revealing their shapely legs – never once did he raise his eyes; and though the fringe of flowers about his face quivered in the eddies created by the dancing, his long lashes remained immobile crescents on his cheeks.

In the morning I had been allowed to see Beebee. She was sitting cross-legged on the floor of her new home, completely covered by a white cloth. Her grandmother lifted it to reveal her face, like that of a little brown Madonna, and her slender, delicate hands folded in her lap. She had sat as motionless and remote as her bridegroom, and so she would remain until he came to claim her – which he did the very next evening.

This young couple exercised a great attraction for me. I see now that I was observing them, trying to discover from them what I could not learn even from watching Ruth and Paddy. Their lives were more simple, more open. I used to run across the fields, between the crops of maize and yam mounds, to watch Beebee husking and winnowing rice, or grinding fresh pepper, saffron and spices between two stones, or scouring and polishing their brass platters. As she moved her silver bangles and anklets clinked together musically. She was so graceful and assured in her movements, so deft with her hands! Her smile lifted the corners of her mouth and gave an inscrutable depth to her glance. And she looked so very young – it was difficult not to believe that she was only a child acting the part of a woman in some play.

My father had given them a goat in kid, and my mother a hen with a brood of twelve chicks. The goat was tethered near their hut, the hen scratched and clucked to the chicks at its entrance. The cow lowed from a lean-to shed nearby. Beebee's husband crooned an Indian song as he tilled the land, the muscles rippling under his smooth skin. He salaamed as I went by, and smiled at me shyly. He had planted a hibiscus hedge around the hut, and he gave me the first flower it bore, with grave and delicate courtesy.

The rainy season came and went. Harvest was garnered and new crops planted. The young husband toiled away at the weeds which sprang up overnight to threaten the sprouting maize with their lush entanglements, and Beebee was now expecting a baby. My mother had given Edith Laycock the material with which to make six little shirts.

'How tiny they are!' I exclaimed.

'I expect it goin' be a very tiny baby,' Edith replied.

It had rained all night and most of the previous day. The dawn was close and dank with vapour as I lay munching my coffee-sugar. Suddenly there came the sound of anguished weeping.

'Jump up, child, and see what it is,' my mother said.

I ran out on to the verandah. There in the misty half-light Beebee's grandparents stood clinging together. The old man's shoulders were bowed low and his body was shaking. He lifted a face ravaged with grief and spoke between convulsive sobs:

Beebee and her new-born child were dead . . . They had come to ask if Laycock might make the coffin.

I who had always loved the sound of sawing and planing was sickened by it that day. For hours the hammering seemed to go on. I fled from it to the stream, to listen to the music of its waters, but in my brain the hammers never ceased.

That afternoon four men came out of Beebee's house with the coffin on their shoulders. The young widower walked behind them staring dazedly at the ground; the grandparents followed after, bowed with age and misery. Past the tethered goat with her kid at her side, past the twelve chicks now fully grown and the mother hen clucking to a new brood, past the lean-to where the cow lowed, along the path between the yam mounds which Beebee's feet had so often trod, down the long straight road leading to the burial ground, the little procession wended its bitter way, wailing as it went, in the slanting rain.

Despite the fact that their marriage rites were performed according to their own to her, heathenish beliefs, it was highly gratifying to my mother that the East Indians were staunch upholders of the sanctity of the marriage tie. It had always shocked her profoundly that the negroes lived together and had children without benefit of clergy, and that when the relationship palled they parted and 'took up' with someone else.

When Morgan was engaged by my father as overseer – Morgan was a stocky negro with a cheerful grin and a pock-marked face – he announced that he had a wife and two children – girls – and a third child was shortly due to arrive. My father accepted his statement at its face value, and Morgan and his family were duly installed in the overseer's quarters under the drying-floor of the cocoa house.

Mrs Morgan, who was by no means in the first flush of youth, was well-spoken and respectable. She kept herself, the children and their quarters clean and tidy. The children played contentedly in their own patch of garden and none of the family was any trouble to anyone. The third child – a boy –

made his appearance a few weeks later and my mother was requested to choose a name for him. Being deep at that moment in *The Prisoner of Zenda* she promptly suggested 'Rupert Hentzau' and Rupert Hentzau Morgan the infant became. He throve and with all the speed that nature permitted was joined by a sister for whom my mother – again approached for suggestions – chose the names Edna May. Mrs Morgan was again well advanced in pregnancy, and my mother had prepared for the emergency with Lily Langtry or George du Maurier as circumstances might require, when some busybody thought it necessary to inform her that the union of the Morgans had not been hallowed by the church.

My mother's attitude underwent a complete change. Indignantly she demanded of my father that either the Morgans should marry one another immediately or else they should be dismissed. My father demurred. He quoted Browning to the effect that it was a dangerous thing to play with souls, and matter enough to mind one's own.

'They appear faithful to each other and form a united little family – take my advice, Alice, and leave well alone.'

Such indifference shocked my mother almost as much as the Morgan's impropriety. She would not know a moment's peace of mind, she declared, while such immorality was allowed to continue, practically under her own roof. Marriage or dismissal – no other alternative existed. At last my father gave way.

'Very well,' he said, 'it shall be as you wish, and I shall inform Morgan accordingly. I only hope I shan't have to get rid of him for he is capable and, on the whole trustworthy.'

When Morgan was told what was required of him he was astounded. He had been employed, he said, on several estates and none of his employers had ever bothered their heads about whether he was married to his 'wife' or not. He was greatly aggrieved and suspected that my father was trying to find an excuse to dismiss him. My father did his best to explain, until at last, still suspicious and grumbling, Morgan went off to break the news to his partner in sin.

For the first time we heard voices raised in altercation issuing from their quarters, and Mrs Morgan hurried into the compound and eloquently pleaded her cause to my mother.

She and Morgan, she said, had lived together for a number of years. She had cooked for him, washed his clothes, borne and brought up his children. Bursting into tears she cried:

'I aint neber go wid no odder man all dese years. Morgan treat me good 'cos he know plenty o' mens would be well glad fo' me to go to dem. If I marry he, he gwine know I caint leave he by de law, so he gwine commence to treat me dif'rent. He gwine give me bad words and beat me. White people neber be de same as all-we. I beg yo', Madam, let we stop as we is. I beg yo' not to make we marry.'

She gazed at my mother imploringly, but my mother was adamant. Sternly she told her that she and Morgan were living in mortal sin and that she herself would be an accessory after the fact if she were to countenance such a shameful state of things continuing.

Next morning, looking sullen and resentful, Morgan asked for the day off to make arrangements for the wedding. He also requested an advance of wages to meet the expenses.

'The fee is seven-and-sixpence,' said my father. 'I will make you a present of that.'

But that was not Morgan's idea at all. If married he must be, then married he would be with pomp and circumstance. His bride should wear white satin and a veil crowned with orange blossom. He himself would grace the occasion in a frock-coat and silk hat. There should be a carriage and pair, and a 'big, big tall cake, an' a-plenty o' Marsala wine, an' a set o' rum.'

My father suggested that all this was an extravagance which the nature of the ceremony rendered somewhat out of place, to which Morgan countered that it was not *he* who had wanted either the extravagance or the ceremony; but since marriage was to be forced upon him he would do the thing in style, otherwise he would become an object of scorn to all and sundry.

'If I aint do it proper, how I gwine keep de respec' o' de labourers? I be dey boss, an' if I aint act like dey boss dey gwine laugh at me.'

Once they had recovered from the first shock of the demand made so unexpectedly upon them, and finding themselves in possession of some money to spend, the Morgans began to throw themselves into the preparations for the wedding with enthusiasm. As a token of her goodwill my mother undertook to provide the cake and to give the bride the price of the wedding-dress.

The occasion when it arrived was a notable one. The bride, encased in white satin and simpering self-consciously under a tulle veil, with sprigs of orange blossom stuck in her hair, was clearly excited, but since the new baby was due with such imminence that it seemed quite likely to arrive before the ceremony was over, her figure was somewhat unvirginal. The two eldest girls, clad in bright orange satin, made a brave show as bridesmaids in spite of suffering tortures from having their feet thrust into shoes for the first time in their lives. By contrast Morgan's resplendence seemed a little dim, for his attire had taken part in weddings and wakes innumerable and bore the marks of the libations enjoyed at each and all. But the drinking of many toasts, mostly straight from the bottle, rendered him indifferent to such trifles, while a full-blown *Frau Karl Drushki* rose in his button-hole, backed with asparagus fern in leafy luxuriance and adorned with white satin streamers, hid some of the drink-stains on the lapels of the frock-coat.

The baby tactfully refrained from making its appearance until two days after the ceremony, by which time both of its parents had recovered from the effects. But alas! events turned out exactly as Mrs Morgan had predicted, and into the formerly happy and contented little family there entered anger and violence, so that at any hour of the day or night the air might be rent with the noise of their dissensions. At last my father was forced to give Morgan notice, whereupon he promptly vanished leaving his wife and children to fend for themselves.

My mother was much mortified; but, as she did her best to relieve Mrs Morgan's sufferings in this world, she consoled herself with the reflection that these were as nothing to what she would have had to endure in the world to come had she not been saved from living in a state of mortal sin.

CHAPTER NINETEEN
The Waterfall

To the east, south and west of the house at Glenside my father laid out orchards planted with citrus, grafted mangoes and other fruit trees, tilling the ground between them and cropping it with cereals for feeding the pigs and poultry.

He also started an apiary with half-a-dozen hives of the local bees. He then imported queens from England, Italy and the United States with the object of evolving a strain by cross-breeding which would flourish under tropical conditions and also produce the maximum amount of honey. He found these experiments of absorbing interest and I was his eager assistant in all he did. I quickly grew adept at the various tasks which bee-keeping involves. I could work the extractor, cut out queen-cells and drone-cells, smoke and open a hive; I even knew how to take a swarm and only my lack of inches prevented me from being entrusted with this. *Glenside Orange-Blossom Honey* found a ready market in Port-of-Spain and thither we despatched our bottles and sections, all neatly packed and labelled with this legend around the figure of a bee poised over a spray of orange blossom.

But I had other interests besides bees. Not contented with having my own fowls and ducks I prevailed upon my father to buy me a ewe with twin lambs. The ewe I named Belle, and the lambs Daisy and Buttercup. To protect them from vampire bats they had to be folded in a wire-enclosed pen at night, and they soon grew aggressively tame, frisking up to me when I mixed their mash and following me all over the east orchard which was now given up to them and no longer cropped. I next acquired a ram, called for some reason which escapes me, Macdonald, and in the fullness of time he became the sire of twins by Belle and singlets by Daisy and Buttercup. Two more ewes with lambs were given me for my birthday and by the end of the second year I had a fine little flock. The question of disposing of the surplus stock now arose and since sentimentality would not allow me to consent to their being killed locally, I eventually obtained a contract to supply annually eight fat lambs to the immigrant ship which brought East Indians to Trinidad, for the use of the captain's table, and before long I had quite a comfortable balance in the deposit account my father opened for me.

The mind of a child is curious and unpredictable. It was strange that I, a particularly observant child with an inquiring mind, should often have witnessed the mating of the livestock at Glenside yet never apparently wondered about the meaning of the process. It does not seem to have struck me as particularly different from any other bodily activity – just as a part of everyday life. There was nothing to underline sex, just as there was nothing to underline the passing of time. The hours between waking and sleeping represented a span crowded with incident; touched with magic and mystery, and a sense of wonder rather than of speculation.

My father meanwhile had decided to take over my neglected education. After our early morning tour of the plantation, which was over by nine o'clock, and a glass of coconut water and a biscuit, we would sit on opposite sides of a table on one of the verandahs, and lessons would begin. They were not a success. I was not a satisfactory pupil, and my father, despite the wide range of his learning, was not cut out to be a teacher. That companionship which formed so vital a link between us, my swift response to the hundred and one things he taught me unintentionally during the other hours of the day, dried up entirely the moment we sat down at that table and faced the pile of school books on it: the whole process bored us both.

My father strove hard to conceal his boredom. I made no attempt to conceal mine. It settled on me like a leaden weight. My attention wandered, was caught and held by the drift of clouds in the sky, by the rustle of leaves in the trees, by the flight of birds, or by some movement in the grass. My father would rebuke me. I would make an effort to collect myself, but in a few minutes my mind would again be miles away. Presently cunning came to my aid, and I grew expert in the sidetracking of my father away from the subject in hand, and on to one which interested both him and me; and in this way, with subtle promptings now and then, I could sometimes keep him talking till noon came, bringing with it that release for which we both longed. As a result I could have passed an examination on the life history of the honey bee with flying colours; I knew considerably more than the average person about astronomy and geology, and I could have held my own in a company of planters upon all questions relating to the production of cocoa; but on the subjects usually associated with the education of the young my ignorance remained abysmal.

My mother, however, with an eye to my future, insisted that I should acquire at least one accomplishment proper to a young lady, so every Wednesday I went to Port-of-Spain for a music lesson, while for an hour each day I had to practise at the piano. The practising I disliked, but I enjoyed the weekly trip to town. I travelled up with Jim and Gareth, who put me on one of the new electric trams in the care of the conductor. I got off at the bottom of Stanmore Avenue where Miss Geldnicht, my music mistress, lived, and walked the few yards to her house. When my lesson was over Estelle would be waiting to take me to Ruth's house, and she and I always met with great pleasure and animation. I remained at Ruth's until it was time to catch the four o'clock tram back to the station, where I met my brothers and we all travelled home together.

In every yard of its erratic course our stream was a thing of beauty and delight. Its variety of mood and form was infinite. Here it laughed and chattered over a narrow bed of rounded pebbles; there it spread itself widely to glide with scarcely perceptible motion over white sands, before suddenly hurling itself forward impetuously, undercutting the roots of trees, and moving, dark and inscrutable, in their shadow. Then it grew blithe and frolicsome again, singing as it threaded a dimpling course between great boulders, until at last it tumbled between two rocks in a glittering cascade into a deep pool far below.

On the very lip of this pool a flat slab of rock patterned with mosses and ferns, the fronds of which quivered in the cool breath of the waterfall, provided a terrace just large enough for me to lie upon. Miniature beaches, boulders, and a cave – the last home of my little people – surrounded the pool, and between and inside them, amid a trembling of fern leaves, grew lords-and-ladies. Tall trees, festooned with creepers, towered skywards, arching over the plumed heads of bamboos whose narrow, blade-like leaves trailed their tips daintily in the water. Into the clear blue depths I dived to swim behind the waterfall, the force of its descent making me gasp for breath, and gaze upward at its sparkling arc edged with rainbows, and at the fragile little plants that grew so perilously at its sides.

As I lay on my terrace scents and sounds filled the air; the smell of humus and moving water, of unseen flowers; the sound of moving wings and minute voices, of the tumbling cascade and whispering leaves. The diaphanous wings of dragonflies questing hither and thither were like splinters of glass; kingfishers flashed up and down stream, alighting briefly on accustomed twigs to eye the waters for fish; deer, moving like timid shadows between the tree trunks, stepped delicately down to drink; and once I saw a sloth, its young one clinging to its neck, move slowly, slowly, upside-down along a branch.

My mother found herself far more contented with rural life than she expected. As I have said she was warmly interested in our East Indian tenants, and it was not long before they discovered – though they never exploited – her unfailing sympathy in times of trouble. For instance there was one old couple who, while they contrived to till their land and sell its produce, were doing so under increasing difficulties; for the husband was going blind with cataract, and his wife becoming unfit to carry the heavy baskets of vegetables to market. When she discovered this my mother got the medical officer, who, with his wife, was a great friend of ours, to treat the old man at our house until it was time for him to be operated upon, which saved him trudging six miles to the hospital; and she put our donkey-cart at the disposal of the old man's wife to take her to market. When the operation restored the old man's sight the gratitude of both was unbounded.

Her rose garden was one of my mother's principal sources of happiness. The love of flowers was deeply implanted in her, and as she sat in her chair reading or sewing she would be continually lifting her eyes to the roses and letting her glance linger lovingly upon them.

I know that sometimes she hankered wistfully after those social occasions in Port-of-Spain which had been so much to her taste: the hour's *tête-à-tête* with an intimate friend of a morning; the afternoons which brought callers, or when after driving out in the carriage to leave cards where they were due, she would go once round the Savannah and, if the Constabulary Band were playing in the gardens of Government House, pull up among the other carriages near the bandstand, there to exchange bows and smiles and to become one with the other ladies reclining in open Victorias, making a charming and elegant picture, through which the gentlemen moved on foot paying their respects.

Yet, though she missed these and other delights, she did not allow the loss to spoil her enjoyment of the present. Her Sunday luncheons became famous. They occupied her mind for days in advance – indeed many of them were planned for much further ahead. Sucking pigs were marked down at birth; cockerels were caponised; the local hunters were told to provide venison, *quenk*, or some other game by a certain date. Outside in the compound were pigeon cotes full of succulent squabs and a whole array of hutches and enclosures in which various prospective victims were in process of fattening: turkeys, ducks, chickens and even the noisy guinea-fowl which had helped to drive my father out of our old home; land-turtles and sea-turtles; and dozens of crabs being fed on a special diet which gave their flesh a particularly delicate flavour.

As for my father, in the opening up of this new life for himself he had left his study and all it contained behind, though he was to return to it later – but that is another story. Hitherto his life had been the sedentary one of a scholar and

he had shunned social distractions; now those years of transi-
tion between middle life and old age had brought with them,
as is so often the case, a desire for more active interests. To the
astonishment of us all he even allowed himself to be persuaded into joining the local club and attending cricket
matches and tennis tournaments, into going to garden parties
and even, on occasion, into dining out. Wherever he went he
was made much of, and the flattering attentions he received
evoked in response a wholly delighted, rather ingenuous
animation. For him, I know, those years at Glenside were the
very happiest in his life.

He particularly enjoyed visiting the few sugar plantations
in the neighbourhood which still remained in private hands,
some, indeed, still in the possession of the families which had
originally built them. Here, in these beautiful old homes the
traditional life of the West Indies still lingered, and hospitality
prevailed as of yore. Perhaps our favourite was Orange
Grove. On immense tessellated verandahs deep lounge
chairs invited ease, while retainers who had spent a life-time
in the service of the family carried around immense
Sheffield-plate salvers weighed down with tumblers of Planters' punch. At dinner an almost 18th-century elegance
reigned and afterwards the young people would group themselves round the piano, while their elders chatted upon the
verandah and grew nostalgic. Sometimes the furniture would
be pushed against the walls and young and old would waltz
to the music of Johann Strauss; while at 'crop-over' dances,
when the sugar harvest was complete, there was that feeling
of release from work that men and women have enjoyed
down the ages since the rites of Demeter.

The guests at all these functions would often have come
many miles, but they no longer arrived, as they would have
done in my grandparents early days, on horse-back with their
gala attire in a basket strapped to the back of a mule ridden by
an attendant; for now there were roads in most places where
formerly there had been merely bridle-tracks, so that they
could come by carriage ready dressed for the occasion.

At first my mother found it hard to get used to the fact that,
where distances between friends' houses in Port-of-Spain
were measured in yards, here in the country they were meas-

ured in miles; and my father, who regarded unpunctuality as the worst form of ill-manners, had the greatest difficulty in inducing her to begin dressing in good time. A quarter of an hour before they were due to start he, already dressed, would be pacing the verandah watch in hand, calling to her at frequent intervals:

'Alice, you have exactly ten minutes more. How are you getting on?'

'As fast as I can . . . Edith *do* hold that lamp steady! You'll tip it over one of these days, then we shall have the house on fire . . . I said my *high* tortoiseshell comb, *not* that one! . . .'

'Alice, you have now only five minutes. It's time I put your shoes on. Are you ready?'

'Just one moment, Lechmere, please! Edith, the rose for my corsage . . . fan . . . gloves . . .!

'Alice, I'm coming in now. We must start in exactly three minutes.'

He would firmly enter the bedroom. Still fluttering the powder-puff over her face and shoulders with one hand and shaking some eau-de-Cologne on to a handkerchief with the other, my mother would sink into a chair, and my father, going down on one knee, would put on her feet the pair of shoes he had chosen for her to wear. Then, snatching up her fan and gloves, grasping the cloak Edith was holding, craning to get a final glimpse of herself in the mirror and looking as tense as though she were going to a dentist rather than to a party, my mother would tap hurriedly after my father's retreating form. But once seated in the carriage all her perturbation would evaporate; she would lean back contentedly and, as she coaxed on her long gloves, her mind was already busy with the entertainment ahead, wondering who would be there, what they would be wearing and what gastronomic delights they might encounter.

Our sojourn at Glenside coincided with the Boer War and I remember being one of a party of children enrolled to sell programmes at a concert in aid of war funds. I shall never forget the enthusiasm displayed on that occasion. The hall was packed, with people squeezed together on the window-sills and jammed against the walls. With voices choked with emotion all sang *Good-bye, Dolly Grey* and *Good-bye, my Blue-bell*; all roared out the chorus of Kipling's *Absent-Minded Beg-gar*; and when, with faces flushed with loyal sentiment and eyes unnaturally bright, the whole assembly joined in *The Soldiers of the Queen*, the shillings cascaded into the tam-bourines we children were holding. At the end of the song men's voices shouted hoarsely from every side: 'God save the Queen! . . . God save the Queen!', and the National Anthem was a thunderous finale.

Then came the Queen's death . . . It is impossible for any-one of today to realise the magic of Queen Victoria's name; the respect, the awe, and, indeed, the love, in which she was held, or the profound sense of doom her death evoked. When she died few could remember any other occupant of the throne; she seemed to have reigned from time immemorial and to symbolise in her person all those qualities for which England stood, all the achievements of which she was still rightly proud. To everyone of her subjects as they donned their mourning her death came as a personal bereavement, and something more: for all knew that they were mourning not only the passing of a great Queen, but of an entire epoch.

The negroes composed and chanted a dirge.

> *Nineteen-hundred-an'-one when de bells commence to toll*
> *Nineteen-hundred-an'-one when de bells commence to toll*
> *Queen Victoria be gone fo' ever*
> *May she res' in peace.*
> *Queen Victoria be gone fo' ever*
> *An' she be our true Queen.*

The following year there occurred, close to our own shores, a disaster that shocked the world. I recall the evening clearly: we were driving home from a visit to some friends and, as the sun set, the entire sky grew lurid, and all the countryside was bathed in a strange unearthly glare. The air was hot and stifling – and when we reached home we noticed that over all the furniture lay a thin film of dust . . .

Next day we learned of the eruption of Mont Pelée, in the French island of Martinique, which, in an instant of time, had blotted out the city of St. Pierre, fairest in all the West Indies, burying every man, woman and child in it beneath an avalanche of molten lava and a deluge of incandescent ash, overwhelming the very ships in the harbour while men leaped from their roasting decks to be boiled alive in the scalding sea, so that one, and one only, the *Roddam*, escaped from that inferno and with her maimed and crippled crew took the awful tidings to Castries, St. Lucia.

CHAPTER TWENTY

Farewell, too soon

No sense of time passing lingers in my mind of those years at Glenside. Incidents stand out, like individual figures on a tapestry whose bright background of fruit and flowers, of trees and small animals half hidden in the grass have been woven by loving fingers: a tapestry where, as in Keat's *Ode on a Grecian Urn* all remains in a state of arrested animation, nothing changing, nothing growing older; and I whisper of it to myself:

> *When old age shall this generation waste,*
> *Thou shalt remain, in midst of other woe*
> *Than ours, a friend of man . . .*

But time did move on none the less, and was adding inches to my stature and bringing the signs of adolescence to my body, though I scarcely regarded them. Looking back to those last years the thing which strikes me as particularly strange is my lack of interest in my body. I was only conscious of it when pain forced it on my notice, and this was seldom and usually transitory as the result of some small accident. Save for that brief and poignant spell when I had striven to acquire a likeness to Ruth, I gave little heed to the question of my looks, and as neither my mother nor anyone else displayed much interest in them, there was little to foster a sense of vanity.

I passed into the first stages of adolescence entirely incurious as to sex, no more than casually observing the changes which were taking place within me. Running barefoot about the estate, following the stream, swimming in its pools and wading in its shallows, lying on my rock terrace with all my senses attuned to catch the sights and sounds of Nature I was untouched by any of the soul-searchings, the morbid curiosity, the dreads and distortions, with which the approach of puberty afflicts so many children.

With the advent of my thirteenth birthday my mother began to make plans for my departure to England the following year. I paid little heed to them. The day, the moment, was enough: a year ahead was an incredibly long way off, and it hardly seemed possible that what lay there could concern me. It was only when the coat and skirt, and other garments which had been ordered from London, arrived, that I began to realise how imminent was my departure; and then my emotions developed.

They were confused and conflicting. I had suddenly acquired a hitherto inconceivable importance. I was the focal point of events, the centre around which everything was revolving. Enormous sums of money – so it seemed to me – were being spent upon me. Those 'steamers white and gold' were threshing their way to and fro across the Atlantic carrying letters about me. Farewell parties were being given for me, and everyone had some small present for me.

But all these things, instead of giving me a clearer realisation of what was pending, only succeeded in confusing me. However hard I tried I could not succeed in identifying myself with any of them. Nor could I achieve more than a muffled contact with my normal activities. Zest in them was gone, and my surroundings had suddenly grown unreal, like a stage setting. I felt less that I was leaving them than that they were shedding me.

On the morning of my departure, after I had dressed myself, I stood before my mother's cheval glass and stared at my reflection, feeling more than ever a stranger to my own self. I had never worn such clothes before, nor so many of them. I was wearing my first blouse and skirt: a butcher-blue linen skirt and a white cotton blouse with blue dots, and a blue silk tie. The jacket to match the skirt was already packed. About my waist was a wide band of silk petersham with a buckle of filigree silver. On my legs were black lisle-thread stockings, and my body was encased in its first pair of corsets. This unaccustomed garb represented the conventional summer attire of an English schoolgirl.

'The child has no hips,' my mother had deplored when I had been trying the things on. 'How on earth will she keep up the skirt? It will dip at the back.'

Ruth had been present.

'English schoolgirls don't have hips,' she had said. 'They fasten the blouse to the skirt with a big safety-pin, and the petersham belt hides it.'

I stared at my hair. For the past year it had been allowed to grow long instead of being cut at shoulder length as hitherto. It was now parted in the middle, looped back with side-combs and plaited in a pigtail reaching to my waist and tied with blue ribbon.

It was a comfortless outfit. I felt self-conscious in it. It severed me utterly from my former freedom. Deep down in my heart I felt chill and empty. I had a foreboding that once I had driven away I should never return to Glenside – nor did I – and an empty place within me would never be filled . . .

We drove off with the servants running after the buggy and screaming farewells. At the Lodge the tenants were grouped waving and salaaming. My face felt stiff, and I watched it all as though it were a dream.

Jim and Gareth met us at the station. Gareth tried to cheer me up by saying:

'What a transformation! My tomboy sister changed overnight into the complete flapper!'

We all lunched at Ruth's. Everyone except my mother accompanied me on board the ship.

'I should only break down and weep,' she said, weeping even then. 'You do understand, darling child, don't you? . . . I keep up my heart with the thought that this parting is for your good, and that you're going to live with such charming people and in such a beautiful old house.'

When the bugles blew for 'all visitors ashore' my father kissed me tenderly, comforting me with the same sort of age-old and ever unconvincing assurance which parents must have given to children since the world began.

'God bless you, Little Lass, and don't be sad. Before you can say "Jack Robinson" your mother and I will be coming over to bring you home.'

He was smiling to cheer me, but his eyes were wistful, and I knew how much he would miss me, for I was closer to him than anyone else. A great lump rose in my throat and I had a desperate struggle to keep back my tears. Gareth hugged me and pressed a 'surprise packet' into my hand, which, when I opened it later, I found to contain a golden sovereign. Ruth's cheek was like velvet against mine and the fragrance of her presence lingered with me.

I could not watch them get into the launch and steam away from the ship, but ran quickly up a companion to the deserted boat-deck. Going as far forward as I could I leaned against the rail and watched the anchor coming up and, as it did so, felt the ship quiver into life, while the glittering sunlit water began to cream lazily away from her side. The sun was sinking to the horizon straight ahead, the sky was a miracle of purity – azure and serene – as we slid past the Five Islands where once we had been quarantined – oh! how long ago? – past Monos with its peaked hills and sickle bays, the twist in my heart growing almost unbearable; past Todd's Bay and Pointe Baleine – 'pickled pork and ship's biscuits . . .' The tears streamed down unchecked . . .

Soon, painfully, I was myself again . . . Divided no more in thought or feeling, unconscious of my unaccustomed garb, I was *I*, alone and sailing away. Behind me lay all that I loved and with which I was familiar: home, family, friends. Nothing else held meaning: neither the prospect of Florian meeting me at Southampton; nor the journey in the train through the flower-patterned fields of England; nor the days to be spent in London with Aunt Maria; nor my eventual destination, Acorn Bank at Temple Sowerby in Cumberland, the old manor house in which I was to share the education of the youngest daughter of the family . . .

The sun was only a fiery rim above the horizon as we steamed into the Bocas. As it sank from sight the sky above it was flushed salmon, and elsewhere was a luminous glow like liquid jade. The glitter died out of the sea and it darkened to violet. The cliffs bounding the channel were indigo, the trees crowning them a shrill green. My heart ached so that it seemed the final burden of that loveliness would break it; and then, as swiftly as the fall of a curtain, night descended, blotting it out, the darkness covering me as with a cloak.

But I knew with a clear, nostalgic certainty that now, in that very instant, I was bidding farewell to my childhood; that though I should see these familiar scenes again, and see them with a happy heart, yet never should I see them with quite the same untrammelled rapture, the same pure, unsullied joy.